THE SOLUTION-
FOCUSED
SCHOOL
COUNSELOR

THE SOLUTION-FOCUSED SCHOOL COUNSELOR
Shaping Professional Practice

Thomas E. Davis, Ph.D.
Ohio University, Athens, OH

Cynthia J. Osborn, Ph.D.
Kent State University, Kent, OH

Brunner-Routledge
New York & London

USA

Published by
Brunner-Routledge
29 West 35th Street
New York, NY 10001

UK

Published in Great Britain
Brunner-Routledge
11 New Fetter Lane
London EC4P 4EE

Brunner-Routledge is an imprint of the Taylor & Francis Group

THE SOLUTION-FOCUSED SCHOOL COUNSELOR: Shaping Professional Practice

3 4 5 6 7 8 9 0

Printed by Edwards Brothers, Ann Arbor, MI, 2000.
Cover design by Ellen Seguin.
Edited by Catherine Van Sciver.

A CIP catalog record for this book is available from the British Library.
∞ The paper in this publication meets the requirements of the ANSI Standard Z39.48-1984 (Permanence of Paper)

Library of Congress Cataloging-in-Publication Data

Davis, Thomas E., Ph.D.
    The solution-focused school counselor : shaping professional practice / Thomas E. Davis, Cynthia J. Osborn.
        p.   cm.
    Includes bibliographical references and index.
    1. Educational counseling.   2. Solution-focused brief therapy.   I. Osborn, Cynthia J. II. Title.
LB1027.5.D335   1999
371.4'6—dc21   CIP
                                                                         99-055849

ISBN 1-56032-862-2 (paper)

We wish to thank the following individuals who have contributed to this book. First and foremost we would like to thank Jason McGlothlin, currently a doctoral student in counselor education at Ohio University, for his technical assistance in the setting up of the manuscript. In addition, he has contributed greatly to the editorial review of the text.

We would also like to thank our colleagues within our Counselor Education Programs at both Ohio University and Kent State University for their support and encouragement during the work on this project.

Finally, we would like to dedicate this book to our respective family members. To Vickie, Tom's wife, and his daughters, Alison and Olivia Davis, for their steadfast support, and to Dick Mitchell, Cynthia's husband, for his patience, persistence, and encouragement.

CONTENTS

PROLOGUE

At the dawn of a new century school counselors face a frontier of challenging opportunities. Questions from parents, public, and legislators about school funding, more stringent proficiency standards, and the increasing complexity and intensity of student issues represent but a fraction of waiting hurdles. School counselors have the potential to enter the new century anchored with a strong and solid foundation in the school counseling profession. Equipped with varied interpersonal-relations skills, which are learned and refined on the job and in formal graduate training, they provide a commitment to enhancing the development of young people. The near future doesn't have to be foreboding—school counselors can be reminded of, and awakened to, their potential to facilitate positive change in the students they serve. This can be done in a positive, solution-focused manner that builds on what is already working for the student.

School systems will continue in their perpetual state of flux, as is expected for educational institutions committed to providing quality and "state-of-the-art" services to students, their families, and communities. As a school counselor, however, you represent a resilient and sturdy part of that system (Anderson & Reiter, 1995; Coy, 1999). Who else but the school counselor would be expected to promulgate a vision of the possible and contribute to positive change? Who else would have an understanding of the psychological well-being of students and the elements necessary for a positive learning environment? Whether or not you are convinced, as a school counselor you possess resources and strengths well suited for a changing and challenging future.

☐ More Than You Realized

This book is not intended to address issues associated with the roles and functions of the school counselor. We are confident that you are already aware of all of the demands and opportunities of the profession and your role in it. It is our intention to offer a comprehensive way of shaping your professional practice as a professional school counselor. The adoption of a solution-focused mindset can enhance the way that you conceptualize your work with students, colleagues, parents, administrators, and others associated with the school environment.

What we *do* present is an alternative perspective about students, their struggles, and the manner in which they can be approached. We have found that solutions are constructed from current and accessible resources rather than discovered during archaeological excavations of the student's past. The solution-focused counselor, therefore, is not the product of formal and intensive training that could require a leave of absence from school. Rather, the solution-focused counselor is one who is able to shift his or her current vantage point to consider alternative possibilities. A different way of viewing things is often all that is needed to begin the process of building solutions.

The Solution-Focused School Counselor is intended to provide you with alternative perspectives. It represents a new set of spectacles for those who have become mired by a tiring, myopic, and uninspiring view of the school system and one's place in it. It is designed to challenge you to utilize your existing skills and assets, and those of your students and colleagues, in new ways. Seeing a situation from a different perspective opens the door to new ways of thinking and believing, and can often open one's eyes to the use of resources that had actually been present all along.

☐ Characteristics of the Solution-Focused School Counselor

This book will hopefully introduce you to, or at least reacquaint you with, personal qualities, learned skills, and aspects of your formal training that you did not know (or had forgotten) you had in your possession. Our intention is to make you aware of and to amplify those things that you are already doing that can and do assist in generating solutions to what appear to be perennial hassles and headaches. For solution-focused counseling, you will learn, is not necessarily about practicing a brand new approach—it is about maximizing the strengths, resources, and talents you currently have. Making good use of what you already have not only expedites the process of solution construction, it allows for a more genuine, personalized, feasible, and relevant exercise in your work with students.

To assist you in appreciating what you already know and are doing as a solution-focused school counselor, and to challenge you in your continued professional development, we have identified what we consider to be eight characteristics of the solution-focused school counselor. Some may be brand new to you, others may be somewhat familiar. Regardless of their level of familiarity, we encourage you to use these as a guide for your own development as a solution-focused school counselor. We introduce them here as a means of beginning with the goal in mind—an aspect that is central to both brief or short-term counseling approaches and solution-focused counseling.

1. Informed Practitioner

First and foremost, the solution-focused school counselor is an informed practitioner. This is particularly important in a day and age when professional accountability and credibility are expected, an issue that is discussed in chapter 2. The services you provide need to make sense not only to you and those you serve but, more importantly, need to be justifiable. This entails being able to defend your decisions and therapeutic actions not only to students, but also to their parents, teachers, school principals, the school superintendent, and school board members.

Practicing from an informed position, therefore, means that you know what and why you are doing what you are doing and can articulate this to others. This means that practicing by instinct or from your "gut" is not acceptable. As a formally trained school counselor, you are expected to put your academic instruction to the test and to operate from a theory-based perspective. Formulating a reasonable and attainable goal and selecting appropriate interventions, therefore, needs to be derived from an established body of knowledge, one that is accepted and respected in the field of counseling.

In solution-focused counseling, practicing from an informed position is not limited to knowing the principles of solution-focused counseling discussed in chapter 1. Rather, it also entails knowing who your clients are and adapting your counseling style to fit or match their worldview, developmental level, values and ideals, communication style, and other distinctive aspects or idiosyncrasies. It also entails being mindful of outcome research conducted in the counseling and psychotherapy field (research that is presented in chapter 2) and using such findings to flavor and justify the work that you do with students.

An informed practitioner is guided by counseling theory and outcome research while operating from a reasonable and justifiable premise, interacting with clients and students in a thoughtful and custom-made fashion. Our hope is that as you read and digest the contents of this book, you will be able to identify helpful and sturdy ingredients for your work as an informed practitioner.

2. Intentional About Time

As you will learn in chapter 1, solution-focused counseling is but one form of brief or short-term counseling. We believe that solution-focused counseling practiced in an effective manner is by default brief or short-term counseling. Brevity is implied in solution-focused counseling; the intentional use of a limited amount of time is a natural part of what we understand as solution-focused counseling.

Being intentional about time means respecting the natural time limitations that are a part of your work as a school counselor, and thereby making the most of each minute that you have with a student. It means not allowing one moment to go to waste in your efforts to be of assistance to students and their families. This requires, therefore, much planning and thoughtful preparation on your part, including structuring interactions with students so that there is a definite beginning, middle, and closing phase, as well as opportunity to solicit from them feedback about the interaction. It also entails knowing what questions and reflective statements are appropriate. This will provide students with just the right amount of counseling work they can handle at that particular time—not too much and not too little.

As a school counselor, you are already well acquainted with time restrictions. This is further discussed in chapters 1 and 2 in discussions about the time element of solution-focused counseling and its applicability to the school setting. The strategies presented in chapters 4 and 5 are conducive to the limited amount of time you have to work with students, and therefore can be implemented in a manner that makes the most of each moment you have with students. We trust that as you read through this book you will further appreciate the suitability of solution-focused counseling to the school setting and the challenge it presents for you to be intentional about the time you spend with students.

3. Resourceful Pragmatist

Just as time is used in a respectful and judicious manner, so are the resources both you and your students bring to counseling. These resources include one's values and beliefs, likes and dislikes, ideas and aspirations, language, and cultural frame of reference. Solution-focused counseling, therefore, is not concerned with employing a wide array of sophisticated or "high tech" techniques. These represent unnecessary "bells and whistles." What is used are the existing capacities of both student and counselor (Walter & Peller, 1992); that is, those things that are already present in the counseling relationship, namely, the talents, strengths, and abilities of both the student and the counselor.

For school counselors pressed for time, this characteristic is understandably appealing. Being resourceful and being a pragmatist means using what you already have, rather than searching frantically in libraries or professional workshops for what you believe to be the "right fix" or "correct cure." Often what is most helpful for an effective counseling interaction is what lies right under our noses or at the tips of our fingers. This could include picking up on a student's use of the word "depressed" and asking her to define what that means for her and how she experiences it. It could also refer to another student's dress, posture, or mannerism and using such methods of self-expression to understand a bit more the unruly behavior the teacher has reported.

4. Preoccupied with Possibilities

You will learn, particularly as you read through chapter 3, that solution-focused counseling is about the consideration of possibilities. Solution-focused school counselors are preoccupied with positive change and the possibility of introducing such change to their students. This represents an essential component of any form of counseling, we believe, but is strongly emphasized in solution-focused counseling.

Such a preoccupation is unfortunately not an easy or natural focus for most counselors, whose training may have emphasized a preoccupation with problems and understanding their causes. Becoming preoccupied with possibilities, therefore, requires a definite shift in thinking and a reprioritization of what is important. Maintaining a perspective that positive change is possible for our students, however, may be the catalyst needed to motivate them toward such a goal.

5. Eye for Exceptions

Having an eye for exceptions goes hand-in-hand with being preoccupied with possibilities. As you will learn in chapters 1 and 3, detecting exceptions to problems represents the crux of solution-focused counseling. More time and energy is spent on identifying and amplifying exceptions than is spent on looking for and dissecting problems or complaints. Acquiring such an eye or a perspective does take some time and practice. However, once acquired, an eye for exceptions will become a natural part of your interactions with students and school personnel and will serve as the fuel for productive work.

6. Salutary Constructivist

This characteristic may sound the most foreign of the eight characteristics we present here. It is intended to catch your attention and to raise some eyebrows. We want you to ponder over this one a bit, for it represents an important aspect of solution-focused counseling.

The word salutary actually means "health promoting" and is understood as the opposite of "pathological" or a preoccupation with disease or problems. We prefer using "salutary" rather than the (double negative) "non-pathological." Constructivist, on the other hand, refers to the construction, as opposed to the discovery, process of solution-focused counseling. Solutions are neither found nor discovered, as if they already existed, somewhere out there. Rather, it is believed that solutions are created in the here-and-now between counselor and client, in their therapeutic conversations, during the process of counseling (Berg & de Shazer, 1993; de Shazer, 1991, 1994).

Being a salutary constructivist, therefore, refers to the propensity to build on or to construct solutions from a health-promoting perspective. Rather than looking to eradicate a problem, the solution-focused school counselor is intent on creating and amplifying what is positive. In other words, the solution-focused school counselor has as the goal of counseling the presence of something positive, rather than the absence of something negative.

7. Generous with Commendations

As you will discover in chapter 4, the solution-focused school counselor is generous in doling out compliments, or what we prefer to use, commendations, to his or her students. This, as we note, is done only in a genuine fashion and is intended to propel students toward positive outcomes. Commendations serve to "cheer on" students who are already on the road to successfully managing difficulties; they encourage other students who have become temporarily sidetracked.

8. Cultivator of Cooperation

The final characteristic we mention involves the solution-focused school counselor as the instigator or mediator of cooperation, between counselor and student and among school personnel. Cooperation implies an agreement to work together and communicate at the same level.

The responsibility for generating cooperation lies with the solution-focused school counselor, someone with training and practice in the skill of working through problems and managing difficulties. This becomes particularly important when we broaden our perspective from individual students or groups of students to the solution-focused school discussed in chapter 6. To make the solution-focused school a reality, we contend, the school counselor must assume a pivotal role. This means educating others and modeling for them the aspects of solution-focused counseling that contribute to the generation of solutions, rather than the stagnation of problems.

☐ Shaping Professional Practice

We believe that solution-focused school counselors, by virtue of their embodiment of the eight characteristics described above, are shaping professional practice today. Your salutary and competency-based perspective is sorely needed in the school setting and system. Your keen eye for exceptions, coupled with your commitment to tapping and utilizing the strengths and abilities of your students, represents a refreshing approach in an environment that can often be pessimistic to many. And your ability to generate solutions in a cooperative manner signifies the pivotal role that you have as a member of the school administration.

As you read more about solution-focused counseling and the various ways it is and can be expressed, we hope that you will be able to identify yourself as one who is equipped and ready to positively shape the practice of school counseling today. We invite you to consider alternative perspectives as a means of providing your students and school staff with the ingredients needed to construct the solutions they deserve.

Tom Davis and Cynthia Osborn

CHAPTER 1

Introduction to Brief and Solution-Focused School Counseling

The popularity of brief or short-term counseling approaches in the 1990s can be explained in two words commonly found at the local grocery store or bank: "express lane." Yes, it's true—we hate to wait. The woman in front of us with nine groceries, not the required "eight-items-or less," annoys us. The man in the drive-through bank line who makes three or four transactions on a Friday afternoon irritates us. And having to travel 45 mph on the highway angers us (especially when orange signs warn of doubling fines!). Let's face it—we all want to get to where we're headed quicker, sooner, and faster.

Cellular phones and pagers keep us immediately accessible: We don't have to wait until we arrive home to get the call. Pentium processors and high speed modems now get us online instantly. And package carriers garner customers with ads for overnight and express delivery. No more waiting! We've come to expect (and, at times, demand) easy access and instant service. We hate to wait.

We especially hate to wait for solutions to our problems. Problems delay us. Problems keep us from moving forward. We get "caught" in traffic. We get "stuck" at the office. We're "behind" in school work. So, when an opportunity presents itself for getting to our destination quicker, sooner, and faster, we'll often waste no time in taking the bait and we'll hit the ground running.

Brief or short-term counseling represents an opportunity to arrive at our goals and solutions quicker, sooner, and faster. It's the "direct route" to our destination, not the "scenic route." It helps us get to where we want to go in the least amount of time possible. It's the "express lane" to get from problems to solutions!

☐ No Quick Fix for Me, Thank You: Dispelling "Drive Through" Myths

Brief or short-term counseling is often (and incorrectly) thought of as quick-fix counseling in which clients are whisked through the counseling drive-through, impersonally delivered a generic packaged deal of "McScriptions" (terse therapeutic recommendations such as, "Don't be such a whiner! Just get off your tail and *do* something, and *then* you'll feel better!"), all for the purpose of saving time. Such an approach, it is believed, only patches up or bandaids client or student problems with little, if any, regard for the pressing issues with which the person is struggling. The individual is therefore left on the sidelines with little positive outcome.

A quick-fix understanding of brief counseling, however, is simply an inaccurate, prejudicial, and uninformed view. An intention of this book is to address such myths and to clarify the premise and goals of brief or short-term counseling approaches in the school setting.

The Time in Brief

Brief or short-term counseling often has been defined as counseling conducted in a short amount of time or in a limited number of sessions. Budman and Gurman (1988) referred to brief counseling as any counseling "in which the time allotted to treatment is rationed" (pp. 5–6). Durations of 25 sessions or less (Koss & Butcher, 1986) or a range from 1 to 20 sessions, with an average duration of about 6 (Bloom, 1992), have been proposed as the means by which brief counseling is defined. The majority of interactions a school counselor has with a student, therefore, could be considered brief counseling, due to the time constraints of the academic calendar and daily school schedules.

This temporal quality, however, is only one aspect of brief counseling, and does not fully capture its essence or intent. Not all counseling of limited duration is "brief counseling" (Steenbarger, 1992, 1994). In fact, brief counseling is regarded as "a heterogeneous set of interventions targeted to a broad range of clients and problems" (Steenbarger, 1994, p. 116).

It is a misconception, therefore, to define brief counseling exclusively as short-term; that is, brief counseling does not involve simply the *limitation* of total time in counseling services (de Shazer et al., 1986; Eckert, 1993). Such a limited definition prioritizes technique over process or person (Lipchik, 1994), and is ambiguous, for the very indication of "brief" duration is relative, depending on the criterion or the comparison (Donovan, 1987). According to duration alone, brief counseling could refer to (a) fewer sessions than standard, (b) a shorter period of time from beginning to termination, or (c) a lower number of sessions and a lower frequency of sessions from start to finish (Hoyt, 1995).

Despite the caution expressed here about defining or even conducting brief counseling *exclusively* in terms of time or duration, it is important to note that brief counseling is not "timeless" (Hoyt, 1991); that is, brief or short-term counseling cannot be divorced from an attention to the importance of time. Hoyt (1994) preferred the descriptor "time sensitive" when talking about brief counseling, which highlights the importance of making the most of each moment, without the constraints or "mandate" (Stern, 1993) of structured time limitations.

Brief counseling, therefore, is neither exclusively time-limited, such as in planned, predetermined, mandated, or fixed length-of-stay counseling services or programs; nor is it entirely free from temporal considerations and restrictions. In fact, short-term counseling conducted in schools or in community mental health centers may be unintentional, for example, the (inadvertent) by-product of efficient and effective counseling or the result of a student's decision not to return for services. In such a case, counseling that is "brief" would be so named only in retrospect, a phenomenon referred to as brief counseling "by default," as opposed to brief counseling "by design" (Budman & Gurman, 1988).

Beyond Time

Steenbarger (1992) proposed that brief counseling is best understood as "conceptually planned" counseling, which refers to "the intentional consideration of time limits throughout the change process, from treatment planning to management of the relationship and selection of interventions" (p. 404). His "Integrative Model of Brief Counseling" reflects this intentionality, as well as the parsimonious use of time and appropriate interventions.

The emphasis on intentionality and the wise use of time are primary characteristics of brief or short-term counseling. Students, let alone school counselors, do not have the time to sit down and thoroughly hash out problems and their solutions with someone. Working within time constraints is therefore essential in any school counseling setting, given the limited "windows of opportunity" that are available with students on a typical school day. Being mindful of and attending to the stages of brief counseling that Steenbarger (1992) outlined will assist in making the most of each moment with a particular student or a group of students. An essential component of brief counseling, therefore, is the *intentional* or *purposeful* therapeutic process, a process that is sensitive to the unavoidable time limits of real life, with the goal being the enhancement of positive change.

Brief counseling has been concisely defined as "counseling that takes as few sessions as possible, not even one more than is necessary ..." (de Shazer, 1991, pp. ix), which McFarland (1995) regarded as "no more counseling than necessary" (p. 4). Eckert (1993) emphasized improvement when he defined brief counseling as "any psychological intervention intended to produce change as quickly as possible, whether or not a specific time limit is set in advance" (p. 241), a theme shared by Steenbarger (1992) in his statement that "brief work represents an intentional acceleration of those change ingredients found in all therapies" (p. 426).

Sullivan (1954) was an early proponent of such efficiency when he referred to "psychiatric skill" consisting "in very considerable measure of doing a lot with a very little—making a rather precise move which has a high probability of achieving what you're attempting to achieve, with a minimum of time and words" (p. 224). That is the essence of brief or short-term counseling (amazing, isn't it, that it was verbalized more than 40 years ago!)—doing a lot with very little: not skimping on services; not withholding important and humanistic care from the students who need it; rather, providing the most essential and helpful forms of care in as short an amount of time possible, because of one's intentional and purposeful commitment to the positive change process. Cutting to the chase without skimping on concern and care for the student—this is brief counseling at its best.

Brief or short-term counseling, therefore, is really a client-centered and humanistic approach. This means, it is focused on respectfully addressing the needs of the student with a commitment to eliciting and identifying such needs and their solutions in an efficient manner.

☐ Active Ingredients of Brief Counseling

Several authors have attempted to capture the key ingredients of brief or short-term counseling through the years, and a sample of these is depicted in Table 1.1. Koss and Butcher (1986) were some of the first to name specific characteristics, and these are frequently referred to today as the foundational descriptors of brief or short-term counseling. Bloom (1992) narrowed these to five components, which include the salient features of being structured, time-sensitive, active, and clearly focused. More recently, Koss and Shiang (1994) delineated five counselor actions, or "technical behaviors," that are regarded as instrumental in brief counseling, which overlap and highlight the characteristics already outlined.

Specifically within the school setting, Bruce (1995) has developed a "Brief Counseling Model," which relies on "four specific components

Table 1.1. Characteristics of brief counseling

Koss and Butcher (1986)

1. Time is limited.
2. Goals for counseling are limited.
3. A strong working alliance is developed.
4. The focus of counseling is maintained throughout the process.
5. There is a high level of counselor activity.
6. The counselor remains flexible.
7. Interventions are introduced promptly.
8. Assessments are conducted early and rapidly.
9. Clients are encouraged to express their feelings.

Bloom (1992, 1997)

1. Interventions are introduced promptly.
2. There is a relatively high level of counselor activity.
3. Specific but limited goals are established.
4. A clear focus for counseling is identified and maintained.
5. A time limit for the counseling process is set.

Koss and Shiang (1994)

1. The focus of counseling is clear and is maintained.
2. There is a high level of counselor activity.
3. The counselor remains flexible.
4. Interventions are introduced promptly.
5. Termination is addressed early and throughout the counseling process.

Bruce (1995)

1. Counselor and student establish a strong working alliance.
2. Counselor recognizes and uses the student's strengths and resources.
3. A high level of counselor and student affective and behavioral involvement is achieved.
4. Counselor and student establish clear and concrete goals.

necessary for successful therapeutic change" (p. 353). This model, illustrated in Table 1.2 is based on Steenbarger's (1992) work, and it borrows key elements of the solution-focused approach namely, eliciting and building on the strengths, capacities, and talents of students, including "solutions previously attempted by the student, solutions suggested by friends or family, and solutions considered, but rejected" (Bruce, p. 355). In addition, Bruce makes specific reference in Step 4 to de Shazer's (1985) proposition that the counselor may not necessarily need to know all the details or nuances of the presenting problem in order to construct a workable solution. A more thorough discussion of this model and the solution-focused approach is found throughout the book.

Wells and Phelps (1990) proposed a three-dimensional commonality of all brief counseling approaches, consisting of (1) restricted or rationed time, (2) a selected and maintained focus of therapeutic effort, and (3) the employment of tasks, both within and outside of sessions, to stimulate client change. Cooper (1995) considered these three elements as integral to any brief counseling approach, but states that finding a treatment or session *focus* that is collaboratively developed with the student, is the "hallmark" of brief counseling (p. 39).

What is evident from the characteristics of brief counseling listed in Table 1.1 is that brief counseling, by design, is an intentional effort,

---

Table 1.2. Bruce's brief counseling model

Step 1. Establish a working
relationship while
assessing the problem
in concrete terms.

Step 2. Investigate contemplated
and previously attempted
solutions.

Step 3. Establish a short-term
behavioral goal chosen
by the counselor.

Step 4. Implement an
intervention
task prescribed
by the counselor.

Source: Bruce, 1995.

one requiring planning, focus, and an orientation to outcome. Hoyt (1994) emphasized this by stating that "brief or short-term counseling is not defined by a particular number of sessions, but rather by the intention to help patients make changes in their thoughts, feelings and actions to move toward or reach a particular goal as time-efficiently as possible" (p. 59).

Time is a valuable commodity within the school setting, and therefore, must be used judiciously. School counselors, if committed to assisting their many students in attaining positive outcomes, cannot afford to conduct any form of therapeutic engagement spontaneously or without preparation. "Time is the critical element, brevity is the watchword" (Lazarus & Fay, 1990, p. 43), and actively encouraging the student to do things differently is the primary focus (Edelstien, 1990).

☐ An Historical Brief

Contrary to popular belief, brief or short-term counseling is not a new therapeutic approach (Cooper, 1995). Sigmund Freud actually conducted intentional brief, short-term, and time-limited counseling in the early 1900s, particularly in his early analytic work. As the theory of psychoanalysis expanded and became more complex, however, and the goals of such an endeavor became more ambitious, the length of treatment gradually increased (Budman & Gurman, 1988). The emphasis of traditional psychoanalysis on free association and transference—which led to the view of the therapist as a blank screen and therefore, as a passive participant in counseling—contributed to an evolving acceptance of psychotherapy as a lengthy process.

Various treatment approaches were eventually introduced in the 1920s and 1930s to speed up this process in an effort to accommodate a wider range of clients as well as an expanding theoretical understanding of personality and human behavior. The phenomenon of client transference, often interpreted as resistance, was viewed as a time-consuming hindrance to change, and methods were conceptualized and implemented to bypass what was thought to be an initial stalling or procrastination on the part of the client.

An example of such "bypass" methods was the early use of projective tests, such as the Draw-A-Person test or the Thematic Apperception Test (TAT). Murstein (1963) described the intent of the TAT, a story-telling task, as "a short cut for getting at unconscious fantasies, thus speeding up the progress of analysis for patients who did not need or could not afford complete analysis" (p. 14). Brief counseling interventions, therefore, appear to have been designed to accelerate the process of change, so as to avoid what had become a lengthy, drawn-out, and often expensive process. Short-term measures were also implemented to improve client outcome, therapist skill, and treatment effectiveness.

Brief or short-term models of counseling have gained considerable attention in research and practice during the past 30–40 years (Budman & Gurman, 1988; Donovan, 1987; Wells & Phelps, 1990). Contributing factors include (Barber, 1994; Bloom, 1997; Koss & Shiang, 1994; Levenson, Speed, & Budman, 1995; Wells & Phelps, 1990):

1. an increased concern with efficiency and economy,
2. changing concepts in psychotherapy (e.g., behavior modification approaches),
3. disenfranchisement with traditional models and institutions providing psychological help,
4. client preference for treatment providing specific problem resolution,
5. the development of crisis intervention programs since their introduction during World War II, and
6. the documented effectiveness of short-term psychotherapy.

A primary catalyst for the recent focus on brief counseling, however, is the escalation of healthcare costs in the United States today (Cummings, 1995; Haley, 1990; Koss & Shiang, 1994; Strupp, 1995), which explains why brief counseling has often been used synonymously with managed mental healthcare.

☐ Help Me with This, Please: What *Is* Solution-Focused Counseling Anyway?

Solution-focused counseling has emerged in the last 15–20 years as one form of brief or short-term counseling. Conceived and developed by de Shazer and colleagues (de Shazer, 1985, 1988, 1991, 1994; Molnar & de Shazer, 1987; O'Hanlon & Weiner-Davis, 1989) at the Brief Family Therapy Center in Milwaukee, Wisconsin, solution-focused counseling has its roots in the work of hypnotherapist Milton Erickson and family systems theory. The foundation of this approach is the counselor's confidence in the client or student's ability to make positive changes in his or her life by accessing and utilizing inner resources. Solutions are constructed by identifying and capitalizing on exceptions to the presenting problem, rather than exploring and dissecting the problem. The student's strengths and competencies are fostered and then funneled toward the implementation of realistic and achievable behavioral objectives. Noted solution-focused authors, who have written on the application of this approach in the school setting and with children and adolescents include Michael Durrant, Linda Metcalf, John J. Murphy, Matthew Selekman, and Gerald Sklare. Their works, and the writings of other solution-focused practitioners and school counselors, will be cited throughout this book.

The solution-focused counseling model remains an evolving construct (Berg & Miller, 1992; de Shazer, 1990; Molnar & de Shazer, 1987). Elements that "fit" this model are still being identified and added. Early descriptions depict it as a "distinctive synthesis of Ericksonian indirection, an emphasis on functional systemic behavior, and a future orientation in therapeutic practice" (Molnar & de Shazer, 1987, p. 351). While its roots remain strong in Ericksonian theory and its focus still concentrates on future functioning, solution-focused counseling certainly does not lack direction and it no longer regards symptoms, or the problem itself, as serving a specific purpose or function (Cade & O'Hanlon, 1993). This means that spending time figuring out *why* Heather continues to call Alicia names during recess and *what* this does for her (that is, spending time searching for and uncovering the underlying *reason* for how Heather got to be a name caller), is not necessary. The focus, instead, needs to be forward, that is, on helping Heather change this behavior.

Solution-focused counseling works within a highly structured and well-designed decision-making framework. de Shazer (1988) has developed decision trees to aid solution-focused counselors in planning a counseling session. Clients and students seeking counseling services are viewed as "visitors," "complainants," or "customers" and their presenting problem is the result of several unsuccessful attempts to manage difficulties. Symptoms or problems, therefore, do not emanate from sickness, nor are they devised by the student to serve a self-benefiting purpose. Rather, they represent the student's genuine efforts at getting "unstuck" and moving toward positive change.

A Baker's Dozen: Principles of Solution-Focused Counseling

Berg and Miller (1992) have listed eight principles or assumptions of solution-focused counseling, to which Osborn (1996) has added five. These are listed in Table 1.3 and each are discussed below.

1. Emphasis on Mental Health. The solution-focused counseling approach is anchored in a firm belief that positive change is

Table 1.3. A baker's dozen principles

1. The emphasis of counseling is on mental health.

2. Attention is given to the utilization of the client's resources and strengths.

3. The client is the expert regarding his or her circumstance and workable solutions. The goal of counseling, therefore, is determined by the client.

4. Counseling is parsimonious: The least intrusive and the most relevant and accessible intervention is selected first, and then it is implemented in the shortest amount of time possible.

5. Change, particularly positive change, is considered inevitable.

6. Counseling retains a present and future orientation.

7. The counselor and student work together in a cooperative and collaborative manner.

8. The central philosophy is: (a) "If it ain't broke, don't fix it"; (b) "Once you know what works, do more of it"; and (c) "If it doesn't work, don't do it again. Do something different."

9. Problems are not solved; rather, solutions are constructed.

10. Exceptions to problems are considered the building blocks for solutions.

11. Counseling is goal-directed or goal-driven.

12. Counseling is influenced by post-structuralist or constructivist thought, wherein reality is created and understood in relationship.

13. The duration of counseling is brief or short-term.

Source: Berg & Miller, 1992a; Osborn, 1996.

possible. Pathology or illness, therefore, is deemphasized and recovery or progress is highlighted. This is often referred to as the non-pathological approach of solution-focused counseling. "Rather than looking for what is wrong and how to fix it, we tend to look for what is right and how to use it" (Berg & Miller, 1992a, p. 3). Time spent deciphering and understanding the problem or complaint is minimized. The focus is on healthy patterns of living that may already (albeit minimally) exist for the student, and the course of counseling seeks to amplify those exceptions to the problem.

2. Utilization. The client or student's own resources are elicited in solution-focused counseling, an approach instituted by Erickson (McGarty, 1985). This entails identifying and then using the student's own language, frame of reference, logical process, presenting behaviors, and ideas, which set the stage for practical, appropriate, and rel-

evant therapeutic work. "A primary value of a solution focus is that
. . . therapeutic tasks are built on thoughts, feelings and behaviors that
are already used by the client" (Molnar & de Shazer, 1987, p. 357).

The student's strengths and abilities are emphasized more than limitations and deficiencies. Solutions to the problem are constructed
using resources that include: (1) exceptions to the dysfunctional or
unsuccessful behavior, (2) past successes, and (3) the student's ability
to imagine a future when the problem no longer exists (Brasher, Campbell,
& Moen, 1993). These are brought to the student's attention and then
magnified and promoted by the counselor's use of compliments and
appropriate praise.

3. A Theoretical, Non-Normative, and Client-Determined View.
Solution-focused counseling always begins where the client or student
is. Simply put, the counselor takes or accepts what the student has to
say at face value; the counselor must meet the student at his or her
level.

This means the student's needs and wishes are kept central (the
client-centered or humanistic aspect of solution-focused counseling),
and the counseling process and the procedures used are tailored specifically to the particular and unique student. In the process (now,
hold on to your seats, school counselors!), the counselor assumes the
role of the *student* and the student becomes the *teacher*. This means
that in solution-focused counseling you, the school counselor, become
the learner, and in turn, the student assumes the role of teacher or
informant, telling you what the problem is and when a workable
solution has been created.

Whoa! A real paradigm shift, isn't it?! This is what's meant by
client-determined. We are not the experts about what our students
need. Students are the experts on what constitutes a workable solution; they will tell us which solutions fit. No assumptions are made
about the "true" nature of the student's problem; the student's view is
accepted at face value. We, as counselors, do not prescribe solutions.
We generate them from the student's own resource pool, refine them,
and suggest additional ones in a collaborative fashion. All of this is
done in a respectful, yet focused manner.

In this way, an unbalanced, one-up therapeutic orientation is relin-
quished for an egalitarian, reciprocal enterprise. "This notion challenges the prevailing idea that the therapist dispenses wisdom and
brings about cures" (McGarty, 1985, p. 149).

4. Parsimony. Simplicity is the rule of thumb for solution-focused
counseling. This means that the least intrusive and the most relevant

and accessible intervention is selected first, and then it is implemented in the shortest amount of time possible. Time is not devoted to extracting exhaustive details of the difficulty presented by the student, nor to constructing the intricacies and nuances of an emerging solution. Rather, time is used expeditiously by effecting possible change in one area, which some have referred to as "tipping the domino" (see Berg & Miller, 1992a).

An example of parsimonious counseling would be helping a particular student identify on paper the costs (bad things) and benefits (good things) of his recent experimentation with marijuana, and then discussing the answers, rather than making an immediate referral to a substance abuse treatment facility. Figure 1.1 presents a sample of this cost/benefit analysis. Highly sophisticated treatment plans are often unnecessary; simply doing what works is the key.

5. Inevitability of Change.   The expectation that positive transformation can and does occur is the central presupposition of solution-focused counseling (de Shazer, 1988). Solutions are possible because change is ongoing. Problems are reframed as periodic disturbances, as opposed to pervasive and irrevocable impediments.

The solution-focused counseling approach is anchored in a firm belief that change is ongoing and inevitable and that positive change is possible. The focus of counseling, therefore, is on what is possible and changeable, rather than on what is impossible and intractable (O'Hanlon & Weiner-Davis, 1989). For this reason, solution-focused counseling has been characterized as the "counseling of hope" (Nunnally, 1993).

6. Present and Future Orientation.   The primary focus of counseling is on helping students in their present and future adjustment. Students often complain that they are not taken seriously by adults, which translates to not being appreciated for who they are at this time in their lives. Acknowledging elementary or middle-school students for who they are at the present moment, and who they are becoming, rather than viewing them only in the context of their past, signals a here-and-now orientation and a commitment to encouraging growth and potential.

Past issues, therefore, take a back seat to present, here-and-now, who-I-am-today concerns and needs, a perspective Corcoran (1997) suggested is suited for most adolescents, particularly juvenile offenders. Who students have been, the families in which they were born, and the hurdles they have faced in the past are all used to better understand their *present* and *future* orientation. The past does not necessarily determine who I am now, let alone, who I will be tomorrow.

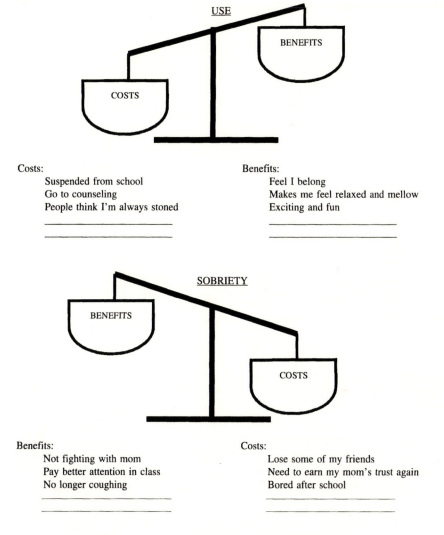

FIGURE 1.1. Sample cost/benefit analysis of marijuana use.

The past is reflected in the here-and-now, and this information is used to formulate therapeutic directives.

7. Cooperation. The student and counselor work together in the solution-focused counseling model. Establishing positive rapport and a therapeutic alliance in the first encounter is crucial. The student's resources are utilized, as mentioned earlier, which "tends to enhance therapist-client cooperation because the therapist does not demand that clients think, feel or behave in ways that are foreign to them" (Molnar & de Shazer, 1987, p. 357). Goals will not be pursued unless the student believes they are credible and attainable. Eliciting student strengths and suggestions and incorporating them into treatment planning and intervention encourages the cooperation of students and reinforces their responsibility in the recovery process.

8. Central Philosophy. Three general rules or guidelines comprise what is regarded as solution-focused counseling's "central philosophy" (Berg & Miller, 1992a):

1. "If it ain't broke, don't fix it";
2. "Once you know what works, do more of it"; and
3. "If it doesn't work, don't do it again. Do something different."

These directives capture the practical gist of the solution-focused counseling approach, and are worded in language easily understood.

9. Solution-Construction, Not Problem-Resolution.   Solutions are viewed as the opposite of problems and are regarded as the substance of positive change and recovery. The solution-focused counseling model, therefore, represents a "paradigm shift from the problem solving approach to solution building" (Berg, 1995, p. 233).

Essential to an understanding of this principle is that solutions are invented and constructed, not discovered (Walter & Peller, 1992). Solutions, therefore, do not represent an already formed, though hidden reality, lying in wait to be uncovered. Rather, solutions refer to the yet-to-be-invented non-problem reality that is jointly constructed in counseling by both the student and the counselor.

10. Exceptions Are the Building Blocks for Solutions.   Solutions are generated from those instances when the problem isn't a problem, when there are breaks or "vacations" from the disturbance, or when there are periods of less intense difficulty. The counselor concentrates on these "exceptional" occurrences and uses these intervals or differences to begin devising with the student a path out of or through the impasse.

Bobby is asked by his counselor of a time in his life when he *did* feel part of a group, in response to his complaint today that he *doesn't* feel that he has ever really belonged anywhere and that nobody likes him. When Bobby remembers his second grade teacher making him feel welcome on the first day of class, his counselor then encourages him to remember that day and how it felt. He is also then instructed to identify some of the things he did on that first day of class to make that feeling last throughout the day. Once Bobby identifies "I smiled to the other kids in my class," his counselor can then encourage him to smile to at least three persons today as an experiment to see if his smiling will have anything to do with his feeling a part of a group at school.

Strategies the counselor uses to formulate solutions are primarily in the form of questions that challenge the student to identify exceptions to the problem. The "Miracle Question" is one example: "Suppose a miracle happened tonight, without your knowing it, while you were sleeping. When you wake up tomorrow morning, how will you know something happened? What will be the signs that something is different?" Other similar assumptive or presuppositional questions imply that positive change will occur, and this forces the student to begin viewing life from a more manageable perspective. Scaling questions ("On a scale of 1 to 10 . . .") force the student to quantify present feelings and attitudes, as well as future potential and possibilities. Responses allow both the student and counselor to better conceptualize the student's present context, and they often represent the preliminary ingredients for determining behavioral objectives. The counselor may ask, for example, "What will it take for you to get from a 3 to a 4 next week?"

11. Goal-Orientation.   Solution-focused counseling, as its name implies, is goal-oriented. Goals are the constructed solutions to the presenting complaint. Several presuppositions underlie the process of solution constructing (Walter & Peller, 1992):

1. there are solutions,
2. there is more than one solution,
3. solutions are constructable,
4. therapist and client do the constructing, and
5. solutions are constructed or invented rather than discovered.

Well-constructed goals, developed out of proposed solutions, have several distinct characteristics in solution-focused counseling (Berg & Miller, 1992a; de Shazer, 1988; Walter & Peller, 1992). These are listed in Table 1.4 and are discussed further in chapter 3. Goals such as these lay the foundation for therapeutic work and serve as a constant reminder that change is inevitable and positive transformation is possible.

12. Post-Structuralist or Constructivist Thought.   The solution-focused counseling model continues to evolve and undergo revision.

Table 1.4. Characteristics of well-formulated goals

1. Representative of the presence, rather than the absence, of something

2. Realistic

3. Agreeable to the client

4. Formulated jointly ("co-created") between the counselor and client

5. Regarded as hard work

6. Attainable

7. Small and incremental at first

8. Concrete, specific, and behavioral, thereby making them observable and measurable

Source: Berg & Miller, 1992a; de Shazer, 1988; Walter & Peller, 1992.

More recently, constructivist or post-structuralist philosophical and linguistic thought has been recognized as an essential component of the model (Berg & de Shazer, 1993; de Shazer, 1991, 1994; de Shazer & Berg, 1992). Simply put, constructivist thought postulates that reality is constantly changing and "constructed," rather than static and discovered. Therefore, meaning is not some already-developed entity hidden away somewhere, but is shaped and developed between people, in the moment, as a result of their interaction and conversation.

A constructivist orientation assumes that there is not a hidden truth or reality to uncover during the course of counseling. That is, the counselor does not act as an investigator or spy to unearth an already-existing objective reality lying dormant within the student. Rather, the student and counselor together, in a cooperative and egalitarian fashion, create reality and construct meaning.

This perspective implies that, in working with students, counselors do not have an already-made "recipe" for solving problems, with ingredients that just need to be "prescribed" regardless of the student or his or her needs. Rather, the constructivist approach emphasizes engaging the student in the process of solution-construction, regarding each encounter as unique, and not presuming a preordained outcome, but looking for new and fresh opportunities for resolution based on the here-and-now encounter with the individual student.

13. Brief or Short-Term Duration.   Solution-focused counseling is one form of brief or short-term counseling, a model that, according to Cooper (1995), is one of more than 50 counseling methods referred to as brief or short-term. Solution-focused counseling was designed specifically as a brief approach to counseling, meaning that time allotted to treatment is not unlimited, but is intentionally rationed. In their work in the schools, Ajmal and Rhodes (1995) indicated that working from a solution-focused perspective is "not so much a case of finding additional time, but using the same time differently" (p. 18). Solution-focused counseling, therefore, cannot be divorced from a time-sensitive orientation.

☐ Summary

Solution-focused counseling offers school counselors and their students a more positive alternative to alleviating discomfort and confusion than the traditional problem-solving approach (based on a medical or pathological view), wherein what is "bad" or not normal is the primary focus, and is pursued, identified, captured, and excised. In solution-focused counseling, students are engaged in a collaborative endeavor to construct solutions based on what has worked in the past for them, what is going well now, and what will be working well at some point (by imagining a time when the problem now is no longer a problem) in the future. In a time-sensitive and time-rationed framework, solution-focused counseling is a competency-based approach, prioritizing and promoting students' abilities, strengths, competencies, and talents.

2
CHAPTER

Brief and Solution-Focused Counseling

☐ New Kid on the Block?

"Brief and Solution-Focused Counseling in the Schools," Sheila mumbled as she read the program brochure. "These workshop people make it sound like they've discovered something brand new. Don't they know this is what school counseling has *always* been—brief?"

"Yeah, it's almost redundant, isn't it?" Ann chimed in, "Brief and school counseling."

Another opportunity for getting continuing education credits had brought Sheila and Ann to the first day of the annual state counselors' conference. They scanned the list of workshops scheduled while sipping their morning coffees. This year they hoped they could find something that was practical and relevant, a workshop or two that offered some concrete and useful tools to take back with them to their respective schools.

Ann glanced at her watch. "Well, we'll need to decide. The next round starts in 10 minutes."

"I don't see anything else at 10:00 that's for school counselors," Sheila noted. "Unless you want to stay here and people-watch, that 'Brief Counseling in the Schools' one looks like it's our only choice. What do you think?"

"Yeah, let's give it a try," Ann suggested. "Who knows?" she said with a wry smile, "If we're lucky, they may have some ideas for our seeing *more* kids in a *shorter* amount of time during the school day and then, magically, *not* feeling burned out!"

The assumption is often made that counseling within the school setting has always been brief or short-term. The time constraints of the academic calendar and daily school schedule, the number of students for which school counselors are typically responsible, and the variety of roles a school counselor must assume on a typical day are indicative of brief counseling episodes. Who has time for long, drawn-out, and seemingly unending counseling-related interactions with students? Ten minutes between lunch and fifth period may be the only possible time. Or a quick check-in in the hallway may have to do.

If the definition of brief counseling as presented in chapter 1 is used as the determining factor (i.e., intentional, time-sensitive counseling that has as its goal the acceleration of positive change within the student) however, such an approach is a relatively new phenomenon in school counseling practice and literature. Amatea (1989) referred to the approach of brief strategic intervention as "a new set of very promising ideas and methods . . . in the schools" (p. 1). In addition, more recent publications in the area of school counseling refer to brief counseling as "new" (Sears, 1993), and appear to make a case for the feasibility of a brief counseling approach within the school setting (Kral, 1987; Littrell et al., 1992)—as if we didn't think that brief counseling wasn't already and necessarily appropriate in the school setting!

☐ What the Research Says

Brief counseling as a distinct and studied discipline, practiced in an intentional fashion, is actually a new concept for school counselors, commanding increased professional attention in the past 10 years (Bruce & Hopper, 1997). We recently reviewed publications since 1980 in the following professional journals:

Professional School Counseling	*Elementary School Journal*
The School Counselor	*School Review*
Elementary School Guidance and Counseling	*Journal of Counseling and*
High School Journal	*Development*

Only 10 articles devoted to a discussion of brief counseling or brief therapy in a school setting were found in these journals. When the literature search was expanded to include the keywords treatment, strategies, intervention, and approach, combined with the words brief or short-term, approximately 89 articles were identified. A research-based approach to intentional brief or short-term counseling within the school is clearly, then, a newly-defined and little understood enterprise.

Brief and Solution-Focused School Counseling Research

Solution-focused counseling has been discussed so far in this book as a form of brief or short-term counseling. It is. We believe, then, that the juxtaposition of the terms "solution-focused" and "brief" is unnecessary and actually represents a redundancy. Solution-focused counseling, practiced in a thoughtful and intentional manner is, by default, brief or short-term counseling. Temporal brevity, therefore, is the natural by-product of solution-focused counseling conducted properly.

In the following discussion of counseling research, however, distinctions are made between brief or short-term and solution-focused counseling. Not all brief or short-term counseling is solution-focused; as mentioned in chapter 1, solution-focused counseling is only one form of brief or short-term counseling. More research has been conducted in the area of brief or short-term counseling than in solution-focused counseling in a variety of clinical settings and with various populations.

Despite its popularity in the professional literature and in practice, we actually know very little about the effects of working from a solution-focused perspective. Most of the reports on its effectiveness have been made by the founders of the solution-focused brief therapy model, clinicians at the Brief Family Therapy Center (BFTC) in Milwaukee, Wisconsin, and students of the BFTC training center. These reports, however, are "substantiated solely by reference to 'subjective clinical experience'" and are often presented in anecdotal form (Miller, 1994, p.21). Claims of its utility and efficacy, therefore, are purely theoretical and have not been subjected to sound empirical testing (Fish, 1997; Shoham, Rohrbaugh, & Patterson, 1995).

Two studies reporting favorable outcomes (namely, length of treatment and achievement and maintenance of client goals) of solution-focused (brief) counseling frequently have been cited in the literature (see Kiser & Nunnally, 1990). These studies, however, were conducted at the BFTC by BFTC staff, were based on "poorly designed" methodology, and have not been published (David Kiser, personal communication, 11 January 1996). A more recent study (De Jong & Hopwood, 1996) attempted to improve the methodological design lacking in earlier studies. While data obtained provide new information regarding the feasibility of solution-focused counseling with a racially diverse clientele, the absence of a control group and the reliance on client verbal report to only one question limits the utility and generalizability of this study's findings. Existing outcome research, therefore, is less than adequate and must be interpreted cautiously (Fish, 1997; McKeel, 1996).

What follows is an integration of research findings in both the (macro) area of brief or short-term counseling, and in the (micro) area of solution-focused counseling. The studies referred to and discussed here are restricted to those conducted with children, teenagers, their parents, and those related to school-based counseling. More comprehensive reviews of research studies in both these areas can be found elsewhere. Koss and Shiang (1994) reviewed the research conducted in brief or short-term therapy and McKeel (1996) discussed the various studies conducted in solution-focused counseling and provided recommendations for future research.

Efforts are underway to further define and investigate brief and solution-focused counseling and its fit within a school context. Recent studies purport the feasibility and effectiveness of solution-focused or brief strategies with elementary and early adolescent children and their families (Lee, 1998), elementary and middle school students (Bruce & Hopper, 1997), and high school students (Lavoritano & Segal, 1992; Littrell, Malia, & Vanderwood, 1995), and adolescents described as 14- and 15-year olds (Franklin, Corcoran, Nowicki, & Streeter, 1997). Additionally, the training of school counselors in solution-focused or brief techniques has been deemed beneficial (Littrell et al., 1992, 1995; Mostert, Johnson, & Mostert, 1997).

Specific aspects of the solution-focused or brief approach identified as helpful for students and their families in these studies include:

1. the cooperative exchange between student and counselor;
2. a sense of empowerment experienced by students who evidenced their own work as significant in constructing solutions;
3. an emphasis on rapid goal formulation;
4. the implementation of clear, concrete, and practical interventions;
5. the deliberate use of planned and time-limited sessions, which both students and counselors reportedly appreciated.

These particular studies, however, do not represent well-designed research initiatives and therefore fail to provide valid or generalizable findings. The two studies specifically investigating the benefits of training (Littrell et al., 1992; Mostert et al., 1997) were based on very small sample sizes ($n = 5$). When a control or alternative treatment group was included (Bruce & Hopper, 1997), it was not clearly distinct from the brief counseling model used. Standardized instruments were not implemented in any of the studies and the methods for obtaining information from research participants were not clarified. Single counseling sessions with brief follow-up contacts actually appear to represent multiple counseling sessions (Bruce & Hopper, 1997; Littrell et al.,

1995). And in one study (Lee, 1998), who the subjects were (i.e., children or parents) remains unclear.

Littrell et al. (1995) discussed the difficulties of conducting research with students in the school setting and acknowledged, as did the other researchers, the limitations of their investigations. Despite the short-comings in design and administration, these studies provide information to assist in further research. Furthermore, they represent initial attempts to describe and demonstrate the feasibility of brief and solution-focused counseling approaches with students and their families. A look at some general findings of the counseling outcome research will identify additional features of effective short-term counseling that are applicable to the school setting. Knowing what works helps us to fashion a solution-focused model for school counselors.

General Psychotherapy Outcomes

Counselors have traditionally been trained in and have used psycho-dynamic, humanistic, and behavioral theories (Kovacs, 1982), which promote the assumption that counselors and their clients have unlimited amounts of time to work together (Cross, 1995; Littrell et al., 1995; Sklare, 1997). Despite the forecast that the practice of counsel-ing will, among other things, become more short-term (Corey, 1996; Cummings, 1995), formal training in brief forms of counseling, within a graduate program, remains a relatively new concept (Levenson, Speed, & Budman, 1995). Many counselors today, therefore, including school counselors, lack such training (Cross, 1995; Koss & Shiang, 1994), and must rely on books, workshops, and continuing-education seminars or graduate course work (which may often be self-selected) for such an introduction to brief or short-term forms of intervention and fur-ther skill enhancement (Levenson et al., 1995).

Graduate training in counseling and other mental health professions (e.g., psychology and social work) has been criticized by certain authors for its lack of emphasis on counseling outcomes (Sexton, Whiston, Bleuer, & Walz, 1997; Stein & Lambert, 1995). Graduate students, these authors contend, traditionally have not been exposed or chal-lenged to make use of research studies that inform the practice of effective counseling. Research conducted over the past 30 years sug-gests that certain counselor, client, and contextual factors contribute to beneficial counseling. Graduate programs need to integrate such material in curricular and program design to more fully equip gradu-ates for relevant and effective day-to-day counseling practices. This book represents, in part, a response to this need.

General psychotherapy outcome research has identified what we interpret as five principles of effective counseling. These principles are that

1. time is an essential element;
2. who and what the client represents matters;
3. understanding and utilizing client resources, particularly who the client is outside of counseling, promotes positive change;
4. client and counselor cooperation is necessary; and
5. cultivating client hope and optimism fuels motivation and a readiness for change.

These five principles are discussed below.

1. The Essence of Time

One aspect of the psychotherapy outcome research that supports brief or short-term counseling efforts is the element of time. In a well-known review of psychotherapy outcome studies (Howard, Kopta, Krause, & Orlinsky, 1986), out-patient mental health adult clients were determined to have obtained the most benefit from counseling within the first three to eight sessions. After the eighth session, client improvement as a result of being engaged in counseling appeared to reach a plateau (see Figure 2.1). Similar findings have been reported in subsequent studies (Howard, Lueger, Maling, & Martinovich, 1993; Kopta, Howard, Lowry, & Beutler, 1994; Lambert, Okiishi, Finch, &

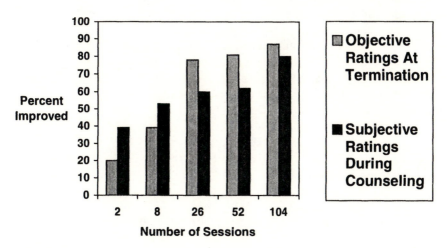

FIGURE 2.1. Relation of number of sessions of psychotherapy and percentage of patients improved (Howard, Kopta, Krause, & Ortinsky, 1986).

Johnson, 1998), suggesting that the first few sessions of client contact are critical for the cultivation of positive client change. Furthermore, if we choose to listen to the results of other studies that report that one session is actually the most frequent number of counseling sessions that clients ever attend (Bloom, 1997; Talmon, 1990), counselors may have only one chance to assist their clients in resolving difficulties. Time certainly appears to be of the essence and first impressions *do* matter!

2. Client Matters

Trying to identify specific client characteristics that contribute to successful counseling is an appealing endeavor. Many researchers and practitioners have been eager to find out if certain factors such as the client's age, sex, racial identity, or socioeconomic status directly correspond to client improvement. Outcome research to date, however, has not been able to extract such clear-cut connections (Garfield, 1994; Sexton et al., 1997). We are left with the general, long-standing conclusion that counseling in general, regardless of the specifics of the client, is helpful (Smith, Glass, & Miller, 1980).

We do know that paying attention to and respecting the client's views about the counseling process contribute to the possibility of positive client change (Bohart & Tallman, 1999; Duncan & Moynihan, 1994; Tallman & Bohart, 1999). Significant factors include the client's estimation of the counselor's level of expertise, the client's perception of the counselor's level of engagement or involvement in the counseling process, the client's affirmation of the counselor, open and nondefensive involvement during counseling, and clarity about the purpose and protocols of the counseling process (Orlinsky, Grawe, & Parks, 1994; Sexton et al., 1997). This means that clients who view their counselor as competent, knowledgeable, and invested in the counseling process, and those who appreciate or even enjoy their counselor, are likely to benefit from counseling. In addition, clients who understand the nature and intentions of counseling and view the process or atmosphere as trustworthy to the extent that they are actively involved in sessions, are apt to demonstrate improvement as a result of being in counseling.

The client's views matter! Tallman and Bohart (1999) contended that "the client is the major change agent in therapy" (p. 103). Listening to and respecting the client's perceptions about what is going on in counseling adds to the beneficial effects of counseling. This means that we cannot afford to disregard the client's thoughts, opinions, or beliefs. Doing so could compromise the outcome of counseling. Taking the client at face value and intentionally utilizing his or her vantage point or frame of reference is crucial to successful counseling (Duncan & Moynihan, 1994).

3. Outside Action

Paying attention to the client's current context implies a focus on what's happening in the client's life outside of the counseling session. Budman and Gurman (1988) observed that one of the value differences between "short-term therapists" and "long-term therapists" is that short-term therapists believe the time clients spend *outside* of counseling is of greater consequence than the time spent *in* the counseling session. Most clients' lives, these authors note, do *not* revolve around counseling, as much as some counselors might wish! That is, what takes place *outside* of counseling is more important to and for clients than what takes place in counseling.

Lambert (1992) referred to aspects of a client's life separate from the counseling context as extratherapeutic factors. These represent characteristics that are part of the client before entering counseling; that is, those things that clients actually bring with them to counseling. These factors correspond to both personal attributes as well as environmental influences, such as personality traits, belief patterns, and family history, as well as current socioeconomic status, social support, and living arrangements. Lambert reports that, based on decades of psychotherapy outcome research, these extratherapeutic factors actually contribute the greatest amount (approximately 40%) to the improvement clients experience while in counseling. Other factors one might think would account for client improvement, contribute less: specific counseling techniques used (15%), the relationship established between the client and counselor (30%), and the expectancy of positive change (15%). Figure 2.2 illustrates these findings.

The implications of these extratherapeutic factors for the practice of counseling today are significant. Of primary importance is working with who clients are, not who counselors think their clients *should* be. This means, for one thing, that counselors begin by soliciting and identifying as much information about their clients as needed, such as their current circumstance, values and beliefs, strengths and challenges, as well as their mannerisms and behavior patterns. This will enable counselors to more fully conceptualize the person with whom they are working, and be able to determine ways to tailor or customize counseling to the particular client, rather than trying to fit the client to a particular counseling approach.

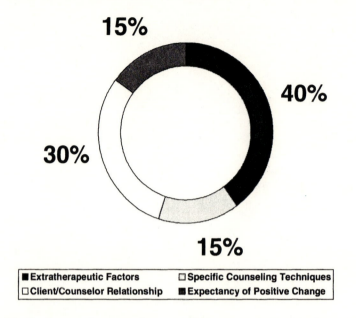

FIGURE 2.2. Factors that contribute to client improvement (Lambert, 1992).

4. Cooperation is Key

The ability for the client and counselor to work in a cooperative and complementary fashion, and to establish a positive working relationship, is an important aspect of effective counseling (Sexton & Whiston, 1994). More than any other factor identified in general counseling outcome research, it is the quality of the relationship between client and counselor that ultimately impacts the effectiveness of counseling (Lambert & Bergin, 1994; Orlinsky et al., 1994; Sexton et al., 1997). In the counseling literature this professional relationship is often referred to as the therapeutic alliance or working rapport and has been defined as "the emotional bond and reciprocal involvement that develop" between client and counselor during the course of counseling (Koss & Shiang, 1994, p. 682).

A primary ingredient of this positive working relationship is cooperation (Berg & Miller, 1992). Cooperation implies that both client and counselor agree on important aspects of the counseling process, such as the specific issue or problem, goals, and interventions, and that both are willing to work together on these counseling tasks. To accomplish this, the counselor needs to invest a concerted effort in setting a positive tone—engaging in an empathic, genuine, and respectful manner with the client; communicating clearly the purpose and objectives of counseling; soliciting client feedback; and encouraging and motivating the client to actively participate in the counseling process. Without the counselor's initiative and attention to these tasks, cooperation and thus, a therapeutic rapport, is not likely to materialize.

Research indicates that, in general, working collaboratively with clients contributes to positive results in counseling more so than adopting a directive, confrontive, one-way or one-sided, advice-giving, "I know best," or expert approach. Demanding client compliance or consistently confronting the client's defenses may actually *increase* the client's resistance and subsequently lead to the client walking away or dropping out of counseling (Patterson & Forgatch, 1985). In one well-controlled study (Miller, Benefield, & Tonigan, 1993), the counselor's confrontational behavior (i.e., challenging, disagreeing, emphasizing negative client characteristics, sarcasm, and head-on disputes) actually predicted an *increase* in the client's problematic behavior (drinking, in this case).

Current work in the addictions field has emphasized an egalitarian and collaborative counseling style, challenging the traditional directive and confrontive chemical dependency treatment approach. Motivational interviewing (Miller & Rollnick, 1991) and motivational enhancement therapy (Miller, Zweben, DiClemente, & Rychtarik, 1992) contend that working *with* the client, as opposed to working *against* the client, is the only way to encourage the client's involvement in the process of positive change. Eliciting from the client his or her version of the presenting problem and stated goals for counseling, and then working cooperatively to address these needs and wants, will enhance the quality of the counseling relationship, thereby increasing the likelihood of client improvement.

5. Expect the Best

What clients expect or hope will happen in counseling is very closely related to the final outcome of counseling (Garfield, 1994). That is, clients who expect or hope that counseling will be helpful for them are likely to improve as a result of being in counseling. By the same token, clients who project negative things about counseling are likely not to benefit from counseling. According to Lambert (1992), these "expectancy factors" account for 15% of client outcome (refer to Figure 2.2).

Brainstorming with and describing to clients the potential benefits of counseling appears, therefore, to be a logical step toward promoting positive client change. Solution-focused proponents (Lawson, 1994; Weiner-Davis, de Shazer, & Gingerich, 1987) have even recommended inquiring about positive change that has taken place *before* the first counseling session. They contend that a significant number of clients can report positive change taking place in their lives from the time they made the first phone call to the counselor to the time of their first counseling appointment. Thus, "a counselor can significantly influence a client's expectation about a preexisting solution to a problem by communicating a definite expectancy (e.g., "What differences have you noticed in your problem situation since you made this appointment?")" (Lawson, 1994, p. 247).

Implications for the School Setting

Effective school counseling in the 21st century will be influenced by both general and specialized counseling outcome research. We cannot afford to ignore what researchers have to say. As with colleagues in community mental health counseling and those in private group practice, school counselors will need to demonstrate their worth. Accountability and intentionality are now the standard practices in managed mental healthcare. If they have not already, they will soon become part of the vernacular in school counseling (Sexton et al., 1997; Sklare, 1997).

Justifying and defending the utility and effectiveness of school counseling will become standard practice (Baker, 1996). Principals and other local administrators, superintendents, parent organizations, school boards, and state and federal associations will be calling on more and more school counselors, on a more regular basis, to show us the data. That is, school counselors will soon have to be demonstrating that what they do is time efficient, cost effective, *and* productive. Working efficiently and effectively, therefore, and providing evidence of such, will be essential. School counselors' jobs may depend on it.

We need to listen to counseling outcome research data, including the data that supports the five principles of effective counseling presented earlier in this chapter. This means, as school counselors, you need to incorporate into your practice what you have read and what you know thus far about student and client improvement as a result of counseling. Specifically:

- Make the most of each brief encounter with a student: It could be the only one you have (see principle 1).
- Honor and respect who students are, especially the resources and strengths they already have and bring with them: These are the ingredients for positive change (see principle 2).
- Peer and point them outside. Imagine and take in what you know

about the lives of students when they're not with you. View them in context and provide for them examples of realistic ways to transfer what they've heard and learned in their counseling interactions with you to the hallway, lunch room, gym class, the bus or subway, street corners, the dinner table, band practice, babysitting, soccer scrimmage, and run-ins with sister or brother (see principle 3).

- As much as possible engage in a collaborative, nonconfrontive exchange with students and their families: This professional working relationship is the arena, the incubator, for the formation of solutions (see principle 4).
- Instill in students a reason to be hopeful, because hope fuels change, change is inevitable, and positive change is always possible (see principle 5).

School counseling is about change—positive change. Integrating general psychotherapy and specific counseling outcome research findings into your practice as a school counselor addresses your needs (e.g., time management), addresses the needs of your students (e.g., making use of their perceptions and opinions), and promotes positive change. Solution-focused counseling in the schools is informed by and capitalizes on research outcome data. It represents, therefore, a timely, relevant, and research-based approach to the development and mental healthcare of students within the school setting.

☐ The Solution-Focused School Counseling Model

Giving School Counselors What They Want

Senior drop-outs, elementary school drug use, high school mothers, and middle school violence. Uncooperative school boards, absent parents, frustrated teachers, and vetoed levies. Natural disasters, ancient computers, cramped quarters, and crumbling buildings.

This list of barriers, gripes, stumbling blocks, and stressors experienced by many school counselors could go on to fill the entire next page. You know the hassles well. Your job *is* demanding and it is certainly not easy. The difficulties you face every day at your school may appear insurmountable.

And yet, it is *because* of these and many other demands that you are needed. Without your presence as a liaison between students and their parents or between teachers and the principal, productive communication would disintegrate. Without your listening and interpersonal communication skills to attend to individualized student needs, problems would flourish and cause greater destruction. And without your foresight, creativity, and strategic planning to establish prevention programs in the district, the schools and the many people you serve would suffer. Indeed, you have been described as "indispensable" in your work as a school counselor (Anderson & Reiter, 1995).

But how does one remain positive, maintain a solution-focused outlook, *and* conduct one's work in an efficient and effective manner in the midst of a barrage of hassles and stressors? How can one, as an "indispensable" school counselor, not just keep a head above water but generate and thrive in work that should be considered rewarding and gratifying?

We propose that by selectively attending to and intentionally incorporating the key elements of the solution-focused school counseling model presented in this book, the work that you do will become (or continue to be) manageable and rewarding for you. The model, in fact, provides you with what you want—the management of: (a) time, (b) student, staff, and school problems; and (c) the cultivation of hope, accomplishment, success, solutions, and resiliency. The model has been described as one of empowerment (Bruce & Hopper, 1997; Downing & Harrison, 1992; Littrell et al., 1995)—empowerment not only for students, but for school counselors as well.

This model has been described well and concisely by Downing and Harrison (1992) and merits inclusion here:

> Solution-focused counseling operates on the expectation that there will be few counseling opportunities, and each must be exploited to the fullest. [Therefore, it] fits into the time-conscious atmosphere of school counseling. It is an active system requiring relatively little direct service time. Because the focus is on solutions, there is little need for fault finding, and this is helpful in working with students who are other than self-referred or reluctant clients. The basic orientation of this approach is positive and thus has great appeal for school use. Finally, solution-focused counseling is dependent upon the use of the strengths of the client, which should fit neatly into the learning-based school model. (pp. 330–331)

Giving Students What They Want

The scene and motions are familiar: A student, Mike, looks down almost instantly and, only in response to the adult's prodding, he slowly, grudgingly, lifts himself out of his seat to be escorted to your office. He doesn't know you and frankly doesn't *want* to be known by you. He'd rather, somewhat understandably, stay in class and not be noticed by anybody. This is an intrusion for him. He sees you as the intruder and his teacher, the one who initially expressed concern, as your accomplice.

Most students who see school counselors, Mike included, are usually not self-referred (Downing & Harrison, 1992). Instead, it is their teachers, parents, or school administrators who send them to your door. Many students arrive, therefore, involuntarily and reluctantly, annoyed that someone would make them come to see you. And what's worse, what you already know about them and their situation (as described by others) has colored your view toward them. You are no longer an uninformed party, an innocent bystander. You have your opinion and suspicions, and these may determine how you interact with the mandated students who unwillingly come to see you. They know that. Students may then feel, understandably, overpowered and outnumbered, with the cards stacked against them.

Barletta (1998) has suggested that a solution-focused approach on the part of the school counselor is congruent with philosophies in a variety of educational settings. Given the positive educative and empowering processes used in the school context, it is not surprising that solution-focused counseling is gaining popularity.

The solution-focused counseling model represents an approach well-suited for students who often may be reluctant and initially uncooperative (Amatea, 1988; Amatea & Sherrard, 1991; Downing & Harrison, 1992; Selekman, 1993). Working with difficult students is discussed in more detail in chapter 5. Solution-focused counseling's focus on quick problem resolution and its emphasis on cooperation can be appealing for students.

☐ Summary

The experience of "quick success for positive change," Bruce and Hopper (1997) contend, contributes to the student feeling "affirmed and empowered to continue constructive action for further change" (p. 182). In addition, soliciting from students their descriptions of the problems, as well as their recommendations for possible solutions, encourages involvement and invites students to assume ownership of their counseling experience. This ownership of problems and their solutions is what is empowering for students, which school counselors have perceived "as the most important feature of the brief counseling model . . . which often came as students took small but meaningful steps in the direction of their goals" (Littrell et al., 1995, p. 456).

Working from the solution-focused counseling model—which is informed by general psychotherapy and more specialized counseling outcome research—is actually attending to students' needs. In fact, this counseling model gives students what they want:

1. brief encounters with you;
2. a sense that they've been heard and their views matter, which cultivates a sense of ownership and empowerment;
3. a sense of connection and belonging;
4. a reason to be hopeful; and
5. relevance, that is, the feeling that what happens here makes sense, applies to real life, and can be transferred to the student's life outside the counseling office.

The brief and solution-focused counseling model actually represents what students have probably been trying to tell us all along: Listen to me, work with me, make it real and positive, and get me on my way!

"You know, that actually made sense." Sheila and Ann were leaving the workshop presentation, their hands full of handouts and their heads full of new connections and ideas. "I guess I didn't realize that there *was* a model to this 'Brief Counseling in the Schools'."

"Yeah, and I like the positive spin on it," Ann said as the two of them walked down the conference hall. "I mean, it *does* make sense to get students involved in their own plan for change, as they put it, and to use the strengths and resources that they bring with them."

"Now it's just a matter of putting this all into practice, right?" Sheila names the projects swirling in her head for the new-found brief and solution-focused model: "In the 'Helping Hands' group, in SADD meetings, with Todd in Jane's class, and your friend and mine, that Mrs. Anderson, Joey's mom."

"Piece of cake, Sheila!"

"Yeah, if only it was that easy," she moaned.

"Well, at least we've got a starting point, you know? At least I know what to look for and what pieces of this model to emphasize, especially with some of the difficult students I have. It was a good workshop."

"Yeah, it was, Sheila agreed as they neared the food court. Now let's grab some lunch and . . . people-watch!"

"Well, I *was* going to say, and then get that solution-focused school counseling book they recommended in the workshop."

"Oh yeah . . . that did sound like a good book," Ann remembered. "Okay, let's get that and *then* watch the crowd!"

From Problems to Solutions: Changing the Mindset

☐ There is Another Way to Look at "Problems"

We so often find ourselves focused on "the problem": What caused it? What brought it about in the first place? What allows the problem to continue? What can I do to solve the problem? What if the problem doesn't go away?

Questions such as these are examples of how we become "problem fixated." We consume ourselves in the problem hoping that somehow if we can understand it, we will overcome it. In the meantime we tend to be doing well with life. Continuing to go along, still functioning quite well, but never really letting go of the problem.

Many challenges that occur in our lives are not within our control, yet we continue to ruminate over them. To some degree, to do this is human nature. However, at times while we are thinking about the problem, we are not aware of the fact that a solution to the problem is simultaneously occurring. There is indeed another way to look at problems. To begin, understand that there are always times when the problem is not occurring, or that it is not so bad. We can change the way we look at challenges in our lives and the lives of students with whom we work. This change in the way we think is the first step in becoming solution-focused. de Shazer (1991) and Nelson (1998) have referred to this as "noticing the difference."

Maintaining Problems

There can be many reasons for people to maintain problems. Often they serve the purpose of maintaining relationships. Walter and Peller (1992) pointed out that in strategic therapy, problems are maintained to conserve a system that exists within a family or group. We can see this in families where a child is an "identified client" and the family focuses on the child's problem. This can also be true for students in a school context in which teachers focus on the problem of a student to the point of not being able to objectively tell when the problem is actually occurring and when it is not occurring. The teacher can be so obsessed with the student's problem, or negative behavior, that he or she completely misses those times when the student is behaving and the problem is not occurring.

Problems are also maintained, often unconsciously, for other identifiable purposes. Similar to the position Dreikurs (1964) offered, children and adolescents have a natural goal of belonging. In their attempts to achieve this goal, young people may engage in patterns of misbehavior or problem behaviors. Children who have a mode of misbehavior or problem behavior are usually pursuing one of four mistaken goals: attention, power, revenge, or withdrawal. Often young people have such a desire to belong that they engage in problem-focused thinking and behavior. The school counselor's goal is to first identify the goals of the student's misbehavior, and then work with the student to find and focus on workable solutions.

- *Attention* seeking can be normal. However, when the attention seeking begins to intrude upon a teacher's ability to teach other students it becomes a problem. The youth may be too aggressive, too passive, or may simply become a nuisance child who is the class clown or trouble-maker. Assisting both the student and teacher to focus on exceptions to the negative attention-seeking behavior is the counselor's goal.
- *Power* can be another way of maintaining a problem. The goal of a child engaging in such a pattern of behavior is to be the boss. He or she will take on the teacher in an attempt to belong. Such power can come in the form of direct rebellious behaviors or in a more passive aggressive means through forgetfulness, stubbornness, and nonparticipation. The school counselor might assist students in identifying how they can engage in positive behaviors in which they can feel as though they have some control over their actions and environment.
- *Revenge* can also serve as a goal of misbehavior. When children feel mistreated or hurt, they may misbehave in a vindictive manner.

Such behavior tends to perpetuate problems and ultimately makes the child very unpopular with others. The school counselor can assist the student in formulating a future-oriented view which paints a picture of what it would be like when the "problem does not exist."

- *Inadequacy or withdrawal* can also contribute to the maintenance of misbehavior and problems. Some students may simply have a goal to be left alone. They tend to be discouraged and feel inadequate. They may adopt an attitude of "the less contact, the better." Such behavior maintains serious problems for the child, such as loneliness, depression, and perhaps suicidal ideation. This is perhaps the most common of the goals of misbehavior. Maintaining a focus on the future and exploring the times when the problems do not exist (i.e, "exceptions") is of primary importance to the school counselor.

It is important to take into consideration the dynamics that may be occurring that help to maintain the problem. To understand that some individuals maintain problems in an attempt to maintain a sense of normal living is essential. Most people are doing the best they can at the time, and defenses, as discussed here, can serve as a catalyst for maintaining problems. It is critical for the school counselor not to fixate on the problem, but rather to refocus the student's attention to what is working, what is happening when the problem is not happening, and to the future when the problem is not occurring.

From Problems to Solutions

Our initial interactions with clients are critical. This is the time that the cornerstone for the therapeutic relationship is built. If we are to consider what actually contributes to client change we might first consider what Lambert (1992) framed as factors that enhance counseling outcomes. These were discussed in chapter 2. They are presented and applied here to the task of solution construction.

Expectancy factors (15%) are the beliefs in change that clients bring to the counseling experience. These expectations might be the result of feedback from other students that your client has heard. They may also be attributed to your instilling in students the fact that you have worked with others with similar situations and that those individuals have done well in finding solutions to their problems.

Intervention techniques (15%) include counseling theories and techniques employed by the counselor. Lambert's research suggests that this factor is far less critical to the positive outcome of a counseling

experience than many helping professionals would choose to believe. Lambert found that the two remaining factors (relationship
and client) were by far the most substantive contribution to change in
a client.

Relationship factors offer a 30% contribution to the outcome of a
counseling experience. Facilitative skills such as empathy, positive regard, warmth, and acceptance are important qualities that contribute
to potential change.

Client factors (40%) are, according to Lambert, the most critical in
the facilitation of positive change in a client. Factors such as the client's
social support system, personal strengths, talents, and beliefs are the
most influential variables leading to positive outcome.

If we can accept that these factors are the major contributors to positive outcome, school counselors must consider a few points. First, counselors
have influence over many of these factors. For the counselor to share
with students the belief that improvement will take place, and that in
fact, it is currently happening, is vital. It is important that the counselor
understands and keeps in perspective the idea that the actual interventions and techniques being used are important, though, as Lambert
(1992) pointed out, are not the most important factors contributing to
client change. The counselor who maintains an awareness of his or her
relationship with the client will go a long way in predicting outcome.
Client factors are critical to positive change. They represent one of the
cornerstones of solution-focused thinking, that is, that clients have the
ability to identify solutions to their life challenges.

Solution-focused counseling relies on a high level of student-counselor activity. A high level of responsibility is assigned to the client. The
relationship is viewed as a collaboration between the client and counselor. The counselor comes into the counseling relationship with the
presupposition that the student brings a host of strengths, talents, and
solutions to problems. The counselor's task will be to work with the
client in a collaborative manner to search for what works. Therefore,
Lambert's (1992) assessment of critical factors that impact outcomes is
in direct alignment with solution-focused counseling philosophy.

Thinking Positively

When students come with a problem to the school counselor, they are
looking for a solution, a way out of a bind. It is critical for the counselor
to "begin with the end in mind." The end is the reasonable desired
outcome that the student is seeking. As discussed earlier, expectancy is
an important factor in change. What the student is expecting is not just

change, but positive change. Therefore, it is important that the counselor begin counseling with a view of the future that holds solutions for the student.

In order to do this, it is important to eliminate words such as "cure" and "fix" from your school counseling vocabulary. As Kovacs (1982) stated more than 15 years ago, "we do not cure, we only facilitate important rites of passage" (p. 159). Maintaining an attitude that your job is to "cure" a student's (or his or her family's) problems inhibits your ability to be of genuine and realistic assistance. Although solution-focused counseling speaks of "miracles," you are not a miracle worker. Your job is not to "fix" things for students. As a school counselor, your job is to assist students in their efforts to work through and manage difficulties and stressors. The sooner you are able to view yourself as someone who helps students *manage* problems, rather than as someone who "cures" and "fixes," the sooner you will be able to work more efficiently and effectively in the limited amount of time you have. Finding a "cure" is a life-long, and often elusive, research endeavor. "Fixing" a problem requires a significant investment of time, energy, and resources. Helping students manage difficulties, however, is a realistic and achievable project.

The central philosophy of solution-focused counseling, as mentioned in chapter 1, is important for school counselors to follow in the establishment of a positive relationship with students (Walter & Peller, 1992):

1. *If it works, don't fix it* (de Shazer, 1985). This very basic concept seems so simple for those in the helping professions. However, in attempts to "fix the problem" the counselor may be overlooking what is already working. An example might be a student, Bob, who comes to you saying that he has been sent by his teacher. Bob has trouble concentrating and staying awake in class. He has a respectable grade point average and completes his homework on time. He told his teacher that he gets up at 5:30 each morning to do his homework. This is a result of late hours that he is working at a local fast food restaurant. The teacher has suggested that the student find another time to study, which will allow him to sleep longer during the morning hours. What seems to be working in this case are Bob's study habits. He is able to complete his work on time and maintain an acceptable grade point average. *Don't fix what isn't broken.* In this case Bob must not focus on his study habits, but rather on those things that are not allowing him to get the required rest he needs.

2. *If everything you are doing is not working, do something different.* So often people will continue to repeat the same mistake over and over again in hopes that "the next time, things will work." A primary example of this dynamic might be a teacher in a classroom of students

with behavioral difficulties. It can become so overwhelming for some teachers that they may be tempted to strike out and yell at students in an attempt to control the situation. This behavior is reinforced when there is some success in controlling the students; however, in those cases where students pay less and less attention to the teacher, both the yelling and misbehavior increase. *If what you are doing isn't working, do something different.* In this case the teacher must identify those times when the students are not acting out, and try to do more of what is working.

3. *Keep it simple.* School counselors spend countless amounts of time and money in professional training at the graduate level as well as in continuing education courses. They typically attempt to stay up-to-date with methods of intervention and skills of their trade. Sophisticated approaches, however, can get in the way of what is really needed. Counselors should assess the concern presented by a student and then choose the least intrusive (parsimonious) intervention to successfully address the issue. Keep it simple.

4. *If you want to do counseling briefly, approach each session as if it will be the last and only time you will see that student.* As Walter and Peller (1992) pointed out, as you adopt this rule you will find yourself becoming more intentional and focused. You will also find yourself looking for those small positive steps towards solutions to your client's problem. As they point out, the desire of the counselor is to see the client leave the session on track to solving his or her problem. A case can be made for the notion that the school counselor was the first solution-focused brief counselor. The school counselor's work consists of many counseling interactions made up of only one session. With this in mind, school counselors are typically solution-focused; that is, their intention is to have the student walk away from the office on track toward a solution.

An example might be a student who comes to you worried about a test that is about to take place the next class period. The school counselor intentionally focuses upon those times when the student had walked into an examination feeling confident and then actually successfully completed the exam. By helping the student focus on what has worked in the past the student is on track to success.

5. *There is no failure, only feedback.* This is a critical philosophy for you to adopt to move from problem thinking to problem solving or solution constructing. The client's response to the counselor should be considered feedback as opposed to failure. Many clients engage in trial and error in their attempt at finding solutions. When a counselor helps the client redirect his or her attempts toward potential solutions, a positive, success-oriented focus is maintained. A school counselor who

considers these rules will have adopted a framework for building a positive solution for students. By doing so, the counselor engages the student in a relationship which will have a higher likelihood of leading to a positive outcome.

Being Student Focused

Many school counselors have been trained in the student-focused, humanistic tradition. Such a mindset is valuable in establishing a solution-focused orientation. De Jong and Berg (1998) suggested that how we pay attention to our clients'goals can contribute to a much higher likelihood of positive change. They describe stages of a solution-building process that set the stage for the facilitative, action-oriented outcome. Although De Jong and Berg do not speak directly to the practice of the school counselor, their concepts can be directly related to the school setting.

A concept they share with other solution-focused counselors is that the client is actually the expert in the counseling relationship. Most counselors have been trained in the traditional applications of scientific methods, using accumulated scientific knowledge about problems and solutions. As a result of this training in the scientific method, we knowingly or unknowingly act as though we are the experts concerning our clients' problems. Many of us have adopted a view that we know what is best for the client and that our perception of the situation is more accurate and valid than that of the client.

In contrast, a solution-focused viewpoint places a priority on the client's view of the problem. The *client* is the expert. De Jong and Berg (1998) insisted that in contrast to the scientific method, clients, not the practitioner, are the experts about their own lives. They submit three ways in which the counselor can move the solution-building process along.

First, they suggest that clients be asked what they would like to see changed in their lives. The client customarily answers with a description of the problem. It is suggested that the counselor accept these client definitions of the problem, as well as the words (or categories) that the client uses to describe the problem.

Second, the counselor interviews the client about what will be different in life when the problem is no longer present. It is important to attend closely to the client at this point, listening carefully and working hard to respect the directions in which the client wants to go. The language or the specific words clients use to express these directions are of particular importance (Murphy, 1997).

Finally, the client is asked about thoughts or expectations about the problem. These expectations speak directly to the strengths that the client brings to counseling and to the sources of information about useful outside resources that exist in the context in which the client lives.

Utilizing the Student's Expertise

Littrell (1998) pointed to two scenarios common to counselors who employ brief and solution-focused methods. In both, the counselor adopts the belief that clients are the experts of their own lives, and that they know much more about their lives and experiences than the counselor can know. Because of this shared belief concerning the expertness of the client, it is critical that the counselor tap into the client's expertise if counseling is to be successful.

The first scenario Littrell (1998) described points to the fact that counselors can adopt the "client as expert" view, but the client is not always ready to accept this point of view. Typically clients arrive in counseling seeking answers from the expert. "Tell me what I should do," is a common appeal of a student seeking your help. The notion that clients are the experts runs counter to the feelings of helplessness and frustration clients bring with them. Often, the counselor is the last resort for students seeking resolution to their problems. It is critical that the school counselor spend time with students helping them to understand that they have the capacity to assume the expert role in their own lives (with your help) to construct solutions.

An additional point Littrell (1998) made is the importance of not invalidating a client's misgivings about his or her own sense of expertness. That is, do not sugar coat or contest a client's argument of not knowing what he or she would like to change or be better. Rather, in a supportive way, it is important to help clients see what is working in their lives and how they are not simply the victims of their problem, but have the capacity to be responsible for those things that are working in their lives.

The second scenario Littrell (1998) described refers to the client who agrees and accepts the role of expert. He suggested that such clients are encouraged to maintain that belief. Such clients tend to be highly motivated and respond quickly to counseling. The two scenarios described by Littrell are portrayed in the following two cases:

Jim is a 14-year-old who moved into the school district six months prior and comes to the school counselor with a story of discouragement. He describes how he has tried to make new friends and has been unsuccessful. He explains how he has attempted to fit into a number of small groups of kids at school, but he never seems to feel that he is wanted.

It becomes clear to the counselor that Jim is learning a pattern of failure, and is acquiring a belief set that tells him that no matter what he does, it won't work.

Jim reports having friends in his former school. He tells how he was involved in sports and band, and how he never seemed to have problems making friends. The counselor sees that this is a case where the client is looking for answers. In his mind he has tried everything and nothing has worked; he is not a candidate for believing he is an expert when it comes to understanding himself. The counselor's role will be to draw upon what has worked in the past for Jim and what is currently working in his life right now. Exploring and pointing out solutions, which are already at work, will assist Jim in adopting the expert role.

Sara, 16-years-old, has come to the school counselor with a complaint of unfairness of a teacher. She describes how she works hard in Ms. Clark's class. She believes that her grade is unjustly low because a substantial part of her grade is the result of a group project. She complains that she has worked hard and done her share of work, but that other students in the group are lazy and unwilling to do the work to merit a high grade. Sara reports that she has always been able to talk with her teachers in the past and always felt that by doing so she was always treated fairly. However, she feels less comfortable about Ms. Clark. She seems to be stuck, but is willing to do what has to be done to find a solution.

The cases above have to be dealt with in two different ways: In Jim's case, he is feeling helpless; he believes that nothing he has done has worked, and that he is powerless to change. The school counselor will have to attend to both his sense of helplessness and assist Jim in focusing on what is working in his life. This process could take some time.

Sara, on the other hand, seems to have a sense of empowerment. In her case however, she seems stuck. The counselor will need to instill a "client as expert" quality to the relationship and help her find a solution to her problem in a brief amount of time.

Utilizing the student's expertise is important to building meaningful solutions for positive outcome. Tapping into the client's strengths will allow counselors to avoid the trappings of assuming that they are the ones who know what is best and what will work for students.

Changing How We Think

For the school counselor to be effective with students and efficient with the limited amount of time available to work with them, it is important for counselors to be intentional about their work. This means that the idea of spending unlimited time with students is a thing of the past. Solution-focused counseling represents an alternative method of counseling students that does not emphasize or recommend exploring the causes of the problem. Causes may be important to address, but perhaps not by the school counselor at this time.

For example, if a school counselor suspects child abuse, it is a professional obligation to report the concern to the appropriate authorities. Exploration of the details of the abuse can and should be investigated by those who are responsible for doing. The school counselor's responsibility is to attend to the student's needs. If indeed, as the expert, the student feels a need to try to understand what the abuse means, it should be addressed by the counselor. On the other hand, if the goal of the student is to feel safe, that is where the focus should be directed. A possible question to ask the student in this case would be, "What is happening when you feel safe?" To make a paradigm shift away from the counselor-as-expert to the student-as-expert is critical to success. It can be a matter of breaking old counseling habits of labeling and classifying students, which in turn often become self-fulfilling prophecies.

Linda Metcalf (1995) offered an example of how a teacher was able to change the way she looked at students:

> I recall a day as a young teacher years ago, when I sat in the teacher's lounge listening to teachers label and classify kids. I remember finding myself depressed and frustrated with some of the negative behaviors my junior high students were exhibiting. I expressed my frustration to several experienced teachers in search of help or advice. I received many emphatic statements such as " yes, he's in my class . . . and he's a terror there too," and " her mother has refused to answer my phone calls . . . one of those families." While I am certain these statements were intended to be supportive, they offered little help.
>
> Fortunately, I recalled a professor from one of my college education classes who once stated that the most helpful thing a new teacher or any teacher could do for themselves and their students was to stay out of the teacher's lounge—lest you become prejudiced against your students! With this in mind and frustrated that I was not getting anywhere talking to equally frustrated teachers, I retreated to my art classroom on a regular basis with another teacher for lunch and conference periods. We soon found that our more positive conversations at lunchtime were refreshing as we talked about personal issues and productive lesson plans. I noticed how I began to feel differently about my students without the labeling from fellow teachers. Thereafter, I also noticed how the students reacted more positively to me when I knew less about their behaviors in other classes. (p. 2)

Changing the way that we think about students and the school in which we work is critical to being an effective helper. Such a change may take time and is often a challenge, but it is possible. It requires a shift in outlook or lens, as the "solution eye chart" in Figure 3.1 illustrates. Take a moment to look for the message in the eye chart. Do you see it? Can you decipher it? To those who have inspected, it reads: "Problems galore need more solutions."

Notice from the eye chart that problems are easy to detect: Their blatant glare stares us right in the face, not requiring a whole lot of visual concentration on our part.

Solutions, however, may require careful searching. They aren't as noticeable as problems (as the eye chart demonstrates), but they do exist and are possible. We may need to take our time, squint a bit, and adjust our eyes before they come into view. Our students deserve our time and concentration in an effort to look beyond the glaring problems to possible solutions. Noticing what is working rather than what is wrong empowers us as educators and counselors.

☐ The Paradigm Shift: Traditional vs. Solution-Focused Approaches to School Counseling

Most school counselors have been trained in traditional counseling and psychotherapeutic methods. Therefore, most school counselors have adopted what is considered to be a medical model of assessment and

FIGURE 3.1. The solution eye chart.

counseling. The following comparison might be considered in the counselor's attempt at modifying his or her mindset from a problem to
solution way of thinking. The comparisons are also found in Table 3.1.

   Deficits vs. Competencies.   Problem-focused counseling tends to
address deficits and weaknesses of the student. The limitations and

Table 3.1. A comparison of "traditional" vs. "solution-focused" approaches
to school counseling

Traditional	Solution-Focused
Focus is on the student's • Deficits • Weaknesses • Limitations • Problem	Focus is on the student's • Competencies • Strengths • Possibilities • Attempted solutions
Student is "sick"	Student is "stuck"
Talk is focused on • Student's problems • Student's past and present • Stability ("stagnancy")	Talk is focused on • Possible solutions • Student's future • Change
Counselor looks for • Enduring traits • Causes	Counselor looks for • Exceptions • Possible solutions
Student is • The learner	Student is • The "teacher" • The expert
Counseling is • Open-ended • Time unlimited	Counseling is • Structured • Time limited
Solutions are • Outside the student	Solutions are • Within the student
Student's uncooperativeness is • Resistance • Intentional, deliberate	Student's uncooperativeness is • Lack of collaboration • Misinterpretation and miscommunication
Goals are • Set by the counselor • Insight-oriented • Ethereal • Reflective/contemplative • Instructive • The absence of the problem	Goals are • Set jointly by the student and counselor • Behavior-oriented • Measureable • Action-oriented • Descriptive • The presence of a solution

problems of the student are the focus of the counselor's attention. Solution-focused counseling addresses the student's competencies, strengths, and possibilities. As counselors begin to modify their attention to what is possible and to the areas of attempted solutions that the student has already experienced, they will see that change is already occurring.

Sickness vs. Stuck.   So often we view students as diagnostic disorders. "I have my ADHD's, my Conduct Disordered, Learning Disordered, Chemically Dependent students." It is easy to label students based upon diagnostic categories. Moving toward a solution-focused position allows the counselor to see the student as being stuck rather then being sick. Most problems that students face are developmental in nature. This is not to suggest that mental and emotional disorders do not occur in young people. However, seeing the problem as a challenge of development rather than an illness puts the student on the road to a solution to life's challenges.

Causes vs. Exceptions.   A counselor operating from a traditional approach tends to focus upon enduring traits and causes of the client's problems. Counselors often attend to what they believe are ongoing diagnostic qualities of a client's concern, focusing upon those qualities which may or may not lead to change. In contrast, the solution-focused counselor begins by focusing on exceptions to the problem. "When is the problem not occurring?" and "What is going well in your life now?" are questions to pose in attempts to identify preexisting solutions to the problem.

Exceptions to problems foster solutions. They serve as the basis for a counselor to assume an investigative role of searching for solutions rather than for causes to problems. This is not to suggest that understanding what has caused a problem is not useful to know. It certainly may be critical to the client in attempts to avoid the same problem in the future. The primary problem that can occur, however, is focusing too much on the cause to the detriment of student progress. Maintaining a view that highlights occasions that are exceptions allows the client to take much more of an active role in the process.

Expert vs. Learner.   Counselors operating from a traditional model tend to see themselves as the expert in the relationship. Listening, assessing and prescribing, and intervening is the mode that often is used by counselors. The solution-focused approach requires that the counselor be an active learner and highly interactive with students. The counselor is the learner who is very intentional as he or she assists the client in searching for solutions.

There are, of course, those situations that may warrant intervention on behalf of the client. For example, counselors must call upon their best clinical judgement when a client threatens his or her own safety, or the safety of others.

Counselor as Open-Ended vs. Structured.   Traditional wisdom would have the school counselor assume an open-ended view of the counseling process. Such an approach would adopt a time-unlimited framework. This is not the case of the solution-focused approach: To the contrary, the counselor will view the counseling process as structured. Time is typically limited and short-term with the counselor assuming that the current session may be the last with the client. Such an approach encourages the counselor to investigate what is working in the client's life and encouraging him or her to explore exceptions to the existing problem.

Answers are Outside vs. Within the Client.   Counselors have typically embraced the notion that answers to problems are somehow outside of the student. This point of view requires that the counselor do something for the client to facilitate change which the client is unable to do for him or herself. The solution-focused position would suggest that the ingredients of solutions are "within" the student. Counselors empower clients by helping them see what they are already doing to solve their own problems.

Counselor Established Goals vs. Counselor/Client Established Goals.   Traditional counselors tend to see the goal of counseling being the absence of the problem. The focus tends to be insight-oriented, reflective, and contemplative. All of these qualities can be valuable, but are typically not enough. The solution-focused approach tends to see the goal established jointly by the student and school counselor. The end result of the goal is seen as being the presence of a solution. In addition, goals tend to be behavior-oriented, measurable, descriptive, and action oriented.

By the nature of their work, school counselors have always conducted brief, time-limited counseling. However, they have not always been solution-focused. To be solution-focused requires a new way of thinking about the challenges the student brings to the counselor's office. It requires a new way of thinking about the capacity and strengths that the student possesses. School counselors must be willing to accept a paradigm shift away from the client-deficit mode to a client-competency way of thinking. To do so accentuates the capabilities and strengths of the client and moves the counselor toward a solution-focused way of thinking and working.

☐ Summary

Solution-focused counseling represents a relatively new and alternative perspective to the traditional problem-focused or pathological view predominant in the history of counseling and psychotherapy. Attention is given to positive or non-problem occasions, "exceptional" times when the problem is not occurring.

Hopwood and Taylor (1993) described their work as solution-focused counselors best in saying, "we do not treat problems; instead, we assist clients in defining and in making those changes in their lives that these problems have hindered. We do this by helping clients think differently, not about their problems, but about their desires" (pp. 95–96). Changing our mindset, therefore, may not imply a new way of looking at problems. Rather, it may mean adopting a perspective that values the client's desires, hopes, and dreams and works toward making such "exceptions" the rule. When we concentrate on looking beyond the glaring problems to "notice the difference," solutions become visible, as the "solution eye chart" on page 43 attests.

CHAPTER

Application to Individual Students and Groups

Knowing to adjust our vision to detect possibilities when problems are presented is only the beginning of solution construction. *How* to make such a vision adjustment and then knowing *what* to do once exceptions have been detected are skills that require practice and refinement.

In this and the remaining chapters, we provide "the rest of the story"; that is, the "how to" of solution-focused counseling. We present specific strategies for transforming theory into practice, with attention given to particular settings and formats. These are not intended to fully encompass or exhaust the array of skills and strategies possible from a solution-focused perspective. Rather, they serve as a good starting point to assist you to work effectively as a solution-focused school counselor.

☐ Specific Solution-Focused Strategies

Genuine Inquisitiveness

You may be one of many school counselors responsible for 200 or up to as many as 2,500 students. Perhaps you have to make do with your "office on wheels" as you drive frantically from one school to another across town. Trying to deal with the pressures of meeting minimum student competency test scores in the district is more than likely not your cup of tea. And knowing how to best educate several teachers who continually regard you as simply the hall pass monitor and the class schedule coordinator is unnerving and exasperating.

In this tedious and often draining school environment there are accompanying lofty and unrealistic expectations for your role and effectiveness, and assuming a genuinely inquisitive stance about the students you serve seems almost a laughable recommendation. In the rush to juggle administrative demands and meet deadlines, students can begin to look alike to you, blending into one nameless, faceless, and often generic young populace and student body. Finalizing the quarterly report takes priority over following-up with who's missing today from group.

To "get back to the basics" of attentive listening and genuine concern for each individual student, solution-focused counseling suggests adopting a "not knowing" stance. This means not thinking of yourself as the answer-bearer or (as discussed in chapter 3) the fixer-upper, and acknowledging that you are not clairvoyant. In addition, a "not knowing" stance places you in the role of investigator, on a mutual mission with the student to clarify the present concern and formulate possible strategies for its resolution.

Anderson and Goolishian (1991) have promoted the significance of working from an inquisitive stance, referring to the counseling process as one of "intrigue" and "mutual puzzling" (p. 30). In his work with adolescents, Selekman (1993) described this as the "Curious Columbo" approach, referring to the television detective who portrayed himself as dumb and unaware to those suspected of a crime. The point was to elicit cooperation from his (unsuspecting!) suspects in solving the crime.

So, when 16-year-old Leah shuffles into the counseling office and shrugs her shoulders about the yelling match with fellow student, Miranda, in the classroom that morning, the genuinely inquisitive counselor wouldn't proceed to interrogate her with "why" questions, nor would the counselor hound her with scoldings.

Rather, the "Curious Columbo" counselor might begin with, "Hmm, I'm puzzled here," accompanied by a wrinkled brow and tilted head. "You'll have to help me out on this one, Leah," the counselor might continue. "You have no idea what was going on between you and Miranda right before you started yelling at each other. The yelling just happened, out of the blue, without warning. I'm stumped about this! Tell me more."

Rather than mocking Leah, this counselor's observations, if presented in a genuine "not knowing" manner, have the potential of eliciting from Leah her perceptions, thoughts, and feelings about the yelling incident. This invited information would also assist both Leah and the school counselor in their deliberations about what to do next. The counselor might then offer the following:

> "I'm really at a loss about what specifically to recommend, Leah. We've had conversations similar to this one before. I've talked with your mom on the phone and I've checked in with your teacher. What can we try tackling next that we haven't tried already that will keep you from having to come down here to see me every two weeks or so?"

Genuine inquisitiveness is not an act. It reflects a genuine desire to understand the young person and to effectively assist him or her in the resolution of a given problem. Its intention is to understand how the problem is a problem for the student, a problem that may seem trivial to us—such as receiving an "A–" on the algebra quiz, or not wearing wide enough bell bottom jeans, or not having a place to sit at the lunch table—but is experienced as a catastrophe for the student.

The student's experience is one that is not our own, one with which we cannot fully identify. Our investigative effort, therefore, as counselors, is to better understand the student's perspective, worldview, and the factors impinging on problem perseverance and those contributing to solution construction.

Speaking the Language

Just when you thought you had caught up with the latest fashion statement, learned to match the song on the radio with the popular musical group du jour, and successfully translated the latest slang word, new ways of communicating among young people debut. While some of us naively think we're still "hip" by proudly slipping in such words as "dude," "awesome," and "whatever" in our conversations with students, the truth is, the language used by students today undergoes a daily metamorphosis.

The solution-focused technique or skill of speaking the client or student's language, however, does not necessarily imply learning the new slang words buzzing through the school hallways (Murphy, 1997). It refers primarily to the concerted effort of placing yourself in your students' shoes in order to catch a phenomenological glimpse of the world from their view. It means meeting your students at their level, working off the same page, and being able to imagine what it must be like to be in their current situation.

Some have referred to this as "joining with" clients, which implies a preliminary working relationship or rapport and a tentative agreement about the nature and purpose of the counseling interaction (Berg

& Miller, 1992a). Walter and Peller (1992) stressed the importance of matching and pacing the student's unique way of thinking and feeling. They specified that "the procedure for doing this is to use [the clients'] language, the key words they repeatedly use to reflect their unique way of thinking and their emotional responses to their situation" (p. 43). Murphy (1997) suggested that such matching allows a collaborative rather than a combative relationship to be established. He provided specific examples of "how not to" and "how to" match the language (i.e., *what* they say) and position (i.e., *how* they say what they say) of teenagers.

Speaking the student's language communicates acceptance of (though not necessarily agreement with) their perspective and the validation of the experience. If 15-year-old Marlon, angry at being suspended for the next two basketball games because of his low grades, characterizes his coach as a "low life," the solution-focused school counselor would respond by speaking Marlon's language: "Okay, what makes Coach Truman, as you say, a 'low life'?" Matching Marlon's words signals an intentional interest in seeing things from his perspective, and further understanding the ins and outs of his anger.

Take your students' words seriously. Their verbal and nonverbal forms of expression are self-disclosures, communicating (to the attentive listener) their values, dreams, attitudes, heartaches, perceptions, and intentions. Join them by speaking their language. Meet them at their level to set the stage for a collaborative and productive working alliance.

Utilization of Strengths and Resources

Ten-year old Kendra was escorted to the counseling office by the lunch room monitor, Ms. Waters, who had noticed her sitting at a table by herself crying, with her lunch barely eaten. Evidently Kendra and her mother had just moved from the metropolis of a southeastern state to a small and rural midwestern town, and classmates had been teasing her about her southern accent.

"I don't have no friends," Kendra sobbed. "Nobody likes me. Everybody thinks I'm weird 'cause I talk funny."

A vital element of a solution-focused posture, which goes hand-in-hand with speaking the student's language, is utilization. Milton Erickson (1954) coined this specific approach and defined it as the involvement and "acceptance of what the [client] represents and presents" (p. 127). This implies that who the client is, what he or she brings to the counseling session, should be acknowledged and intentionally factored into the mix of counseling. This includes specific personality traits, talents, accomplishments, and opinions. The point is to use the client's abilities, resources, and idiosyncrasies in the therapeutic conversation to build rapport, to clarify the area of concern, and to formulate a solution. The advantages of this approach include (1) building on something already known to the client to work, (2) being more efficient, and (3) being more durable (Gingerich, de Shazer, & Weiner-Davis, 1988).

With Kendra, who is shy and has moved from an entirely different geographical region and cultural context, such resources and strengths could include:

- courage and tenacity in the midst of unfamiliarity;
- an awareness of different kinds of people, language, and life styles;
- open-mindedness to different views;
- keen observation and attentiveness;
- an understanding about friendship and the qualities that make a true friend; and
- an ability to carefully select (i.e., to be choosy about) trusting and reliable friends.

The process of utilization first involves an identification and itemization of the student's resources, namely his or her strengths and abilities. Miller (1997) recommended the use of "detective questions" (p. 7) as a means of "detecting" positive attributes previously unacknowledged in the student. Such a process is actually an exercise in reframing, whereby things that appear at first glance as problems or liabilities are viewed from another perspective and framed in another way, and are seen as positive ingredients and assets. For Kendra, the assets listed above are actually a reframing or a reinterpretation of what she sees as problems, such as feeling different from everyone else in school, being a "funny" talker, feeling "weird," someone whom no one likes, and without friends.

"You know what?" the solution-focused counselor asked. "You have a lot of strength, Kendra. I mean it takes a lot of guts to move all the way up here where you don't know anybody, and to come to an unfamiliar school where you feel different."

"I didn't have no choice."

"Well, you may not have had a choice about moving, but it's taken a lot of strength and courage on your part to come to school everyday, feeling the way you do."

"What do you mean?" Kendra asked quizzically.

"I mean that there's something in you that's keeping you going even when you're feeling different from everybody else and lonely. And actually, you have more going for you than you realize."

"Like what?"

"Well, for one," the counselor began, "you've got a keen eye for differences, for different people, and for what makes a good friend and what makes a bad friend. Since you've been up here, you've had lots of time to observe others, to people-watch, as they say. You've soaked all this in like a sponge, I imagine, and so you've learned a lot about how other people act. And you're probably pretty good, I would think, about spotting who can be trusted and who can't. This is a skill, a quality, not many people have, especially not many kids in fifth grade."

For the first time since she started talking with the counselor, Kendra looked up with a faint smile, rustling the tissue in her hands, and slowly began to swing her dangling legs. The praise, positive feedback, and reframing got her attention.

"You actually seem like you could be a pretty good detective," the counselor continued. "I mean, you've had lots of time to watch the other kids here in school and to learn some things about them that they probably don't even know about themselves."

"I've got an idea, 'Detective Kendra,'" the counselor suggested.

Now that the counselor identified Kendra's strengths and assets, the utilization process could begin. The counselor used Kendra's observational and perceptive qualities to formulate a solution.

"Since you're good at people-watching, I want you to put your detective cap on and think of someone in your class you'd like to get to know."

Kendra stopped swinging her legs and appeared to be running down the list of classmates in her head.

"Who hasn't made fun of the way you talk?" the counselor continued. "Who do you think, based on your observations of them in class or in the lunch room, would actually be glad to hear you talk and would ask you questions about life and school down south? Who do you think, detective?"

The utilization process not only highlights non-problem exceptions; it involves the client or student in the process of solution-building and goal implementation. The counselor working with Kendra didn't prescribe a solution that was foreign to her. Rather, the counselor used what Kendra already had, qualities she wasn't aware of, to get Kendra on board as a "co-conspirator" in problem-busting to work through her problem. School counselors should allow and encourage their students to do what they do best, by capitalizing on their strengths and resources. This is at the heart of utilization in solution-focused counseling.

Commendations

"If you can't find anything nice to say about her, then don't say anything at all."

Many of us may remember hearing this adage from a parent or other family member in our formative years. It represents an adherence to politeness, an effort to "accentuate the positive and eliminate the negative." It also represents a pledge of sincerity to interact with others in a genuine fashion.

Solution-focused counselors speak of the importance of "complimenting" clients on past accomplishments and "cheerleading" their recent successes (Berg & Miller, 1992; Kral & Kowalski, 1989; Selekman, 1993). Some (Campbell, Elder, Gallagher, Simon, & Taylor, 1999) have even stated that "in a general sense, all of solution-focused therapy is compliments" (p. 36). Children, and especially teenagers, however, are keen at detecting veiled attempts at praise, those "feel good warm fuzzies" that quickly evaporate because they don't take the young person seriously. Identifying the positive aspects of someone's character or circumstance is central to the solution-focused approach. Doing so in a disingenuous manner, however, is antithetical to its principles, and is actually tantamount to mockery.

We prefer the term "commendation" in our work as solution-focused counselors and educators. Commendation connotes the recognition of genuine or authentic material, the qualities of courage, tenacity, and perceptiveness, for example, in 10-year-old Kendra. The school counselor didn't make things up about Kendra to simply make her feel better. Rather, the two of them played detective by identifying positive attributes in this young girl, reframing what Kendra had thought were negative and handicapping characteristics into noteworthy exceptions.

It is important that we detect such authentic attributes and accomplishments in our students. Simply arriving to school on time or saying, "I'm sorry" to a teacher may represent monumental tasks for certain students. Getting a "C" in chemistry, sitting next to a new classmate in the lunchroom, or staying on a losing team may also represent qualities and accomplishments that deserve recognition.

Identifying these and other relevant commendable qualities in students is not a simple task; it's not intended to be. Campbell et al. (1999), however, have constructed what they described as a "compliment template" with five components to assist counselors in knowing how to structure and convey a compliment or commendation. The components of the template are:

1. providing a normalizing statement;
2. restructuring statements (e.g., assisting the client in finding an alternative perspective to the problem statement);
3. providing an affirmation of the client's competencies;
4. providing a bridging statement (i.e., making a logical connection between the suggested next steps and what was previously discussed); and
5. providing the client with simple and possible suggestions.

Such a template can help counselors break down and further understand the process of providing students with commendations.

Remaining persistently watchful for notable exceptions in students is a humanitarian endeavor, representing confidence in their abilities, as well as investment in their development and achievement. We pay students the utmost respect by intentionally looking for, finding, and then commending them on their true skills and strengths.

Counting on Change

A pervasive assumption of solution-focused counseling is that change is inevitable, that is, nothing is always the same (Walter & Peller, 1992). Students complain, however, that "I'm never going to graduate" or "Everybody's always picking on me," as if such experiences are absolute, permanent, and pervasive fixtures. It is this kind of stagnant or stuck thinking that needs to be challenged from a solution-focused approach. Four ways of doing so are discussed below.

Here-and-Now Focus

One way to challenge such thinking is to attend to what the student is doing in the here-and-now. Since change is always occurring, focusing on the student's immediate or current thinking, actions, or experiences will elicit evidence to the contrary of "always" and "never."

> "Okay, so you're coming to school just about every day and you're telling me you're putting in two or three hours of homework a night even though you say you're never going to graduate. Sounds to me like you're working pretty hard and are determined to get that diploma!"

> "So it feels like everyone at school is always picking on you. It seems to you like there isn't a single minute while you're in school that you're free from being teased or made fun of. You say that when you walk

down the hall, you're teased and that all throughout class you're teased. Is this how it really is?"

This cognitive-behavioral disputation is an appropriate solution-focused intervention when students present a seemingly stuck situation. It is the student's perception of non-change that needs to be challenged because such stagnant thinking breeds complacency or apathy, which in turn leads to inactivity. Proving the student wrong, therefore, or "spitting in the student's soup" (i.e., making the problem unpalatable), as Adlerian counselors describe it, loosens the student's grip on his or her certainty of non-change. It offers a new and fresh alternative view.

Learning to Be Optimistic

Martin Seligman (1991) has suggested that depression is a learned construct or phenomenon, what he has referred to as "learned helplessness." He proposed that how one interprets or explains every day occurrences or life events is related to one's mental health. An explanatory style that is permanent, pervasive, and personalized, such as that expressed in the belief, "I'll never have no friends 'cause I talk funny," contributes to a sense of helplessness and stagnation, that can eventually lead to depression.

But if depression is a learned construct, Seligman (1991) later reasoned, so is optimism. According to his theory, then, persons who explain an unfortunate event or problem as (a) temporary, rather than fixed or permanent; (b) specific or contained, rather than pervasive; and (c) something for which they may not be responsible but something they can successfully manage, are persons who are more than likely mentally healthy and generally optimistic.

The perception that one doesn't have any friends (pervasive), and will never have any friends (permanent), because of the unique way they talk (personalized) can be challenged or at least reframed in the following manner:

> "It seems at the moment, Kendra, like there isn't even a single person in school right now who likes you, and you're afraid that there will never be anyone who likes you, simply because the way you talk is different from how most of the people talk around here. It feels to you like things are never going to change, that not having any friends is all your fault, and that there's nothing you can do about it. This is how it feels to you right now.

"But you know what I believe, Kendra? I really believe that this isn't how it's *always* going to be for you, that what you're feeling now is temporary, and things are going to change for you."

This reframing highlights this young person's sense of permanence, pervasiveness, and personalization. It is a first step in challenging the notion that things will never change and that being stuck in loneliness is forever. According to Seligman (1991), it represents a way of teaching people a new, more positive way of thinking about themselves and the world. And, as Furman and Ahola (1995) wisely explained, "when people are helped to foresee a good future for themselves, they automatically begin to view their present difficulties as a transitory phase, rather than as an everlasting predicament" (p. 55).

Externalization

Another method in solution-focused counseling to promote the view that change is inevitable and that positive change is possible is that of externalization. At certain points in their development, children and teenagers are prone to thinking that the world revolves around them or that they are completely responsible for events taking place around them. Both views exemplify an internalized or personalized explanatory style (i.e., "it's all about me"), which can contribute to a sense of "stuckness" with a concurrent feeling that there's no way out (i.e., "it's all my fault").

Nick was a junior at the local vocational high school, enrolled in the horticulture program. He had been referred to the school counselor by his science teacher for numerous absences from class. He was a short and slightly built young man, soft-spoken and quiet. Although he was polite and cooperative with the counselor, he seemed hesitant about explaining his absences. Only after some prodding did he acknowledge that two popular girls in his science class had been teasing him recently. They had placed chewing gum on his seat, locked him out of the lab one day, and pushed papers off his table.

"I guess I'm just slow and backward," he explained, attributing his being teased to something about him he felt he deserved. "I'm not too smart and they know it."

Nick said he didn't want to go to science class, and preferred to go to the school's nursery instead, where he could tend to the plants and shrubs the program grew.

"No one there pesters me," he said. "It's quiet. And besides, I want to do landscaping one day, not be a scientist."

It was evident in talking with Nick that he identified himself—his being "backward" and "not too smart"—as the problem, rather than a cyclical pattern of nonassertiveness in response to unfair treatment. He lacked self-confidence in social situations and was not able to assume an assertive stance with the two girls in class. He believed there wasn't anything he could do about the situation, other than to slip off quietly to the school nursery.

The school counselor worked with Nick to shift his focus from an internal or personalized explanation of the problem ("I'm backward and not too smart") to an external attribution ("unfair treatment that goes unchallenged"). He was encouraged to see that the problem which brought him to counseling was not something that resided solely in him, but was actually a relationship difficulty, something that involved him and two other people.

One of the first strategies implemented by the counselor to shift Nick's perspective from inside to outside himself was to give the problem a name. The simple act of naming a nagging (and perhaps vague) difficulty engenders a sense of control over the situation. It helps to establish and clarify parameters and boundaries ("it's this and not that"), which serves to contain the problem. In Nick's case, the name both he and the counselor chose for the problem was "late-blooming assertiveness." Not only did this particular name use horticultural imagery to which Nick could relate; it identified the solution (assertiveness) and framed the problem in developmental and positive language, as being not yet the solution. Nick was able to see over time that he had social strengths in him, and those strengths were just in their early stage of development, not yet fully formed.

Once the problem had a name, Nick and his counselor had a focus for their conversations and were clear about the purpose or destination of counseling (i.e., to help Nick become more assertive with others). The counselor at one point used a Gestalt therapy strategy by having Nick role play and then talk to "late-blooming assertiveness," telling it that it was "time to grow up and stand your ground." Talking about and to this newly identified entity helped Nick realize that he wasn't a helpless victim, but actually had some control over the situation. And, in the process, Nick was practicing being assertive! Positive change had become a reality for him.

Presuppositional Stance

In Basic Attending Skills 101 class in our counselor training program, we were (it is hoped) taught the importance of asking open-ended questions, as opposed to asking closed questions (those that can only be answered with either "yes" or "no"). Closed questions stifle conversation, whereas open-ended questions, prefaced with "how" and "what," encourage client involvement.

From a solution-focused perspective, a means of encouraging client involvement and instilling an expectation of positive change is to assume a presuppositional stance. This means that counselors assume or presuppose that positive change will take place in the client's life and is, in fact, already taking place. Such an outlook is communicated in the specific words used. "*When* you tell your mom about your marijuana use" implies that such a conversation is going to take place, as opposed to "*If* you tell your mom about your marijuana use." The first phrase signals action, whereas the second invites tentativeness and may endorse inaction. Students will pick up on the difference.

Counseling is about change. Assuming a change-oriented posture and then communicating this to students goes to the very heart of this business of counseling. Without investing in the reality of change and the possibility of positive change, we do our students and their families a grave disservice.

Highlighting Exceptions

Exceptions have been defined as problem "irregularit[ies]" (Miller, 1992, p. 2); that is, occasions when the problem is not a problem or times when the problem could have happened but did not (Berg, 1994). From a solution-focused counseling approach, exceptions are the ingredients and the building blocks of solutions. They represent the yeast of goal formulation. Without evidence to the contrary of complaints or concerns, solutions cannot be constructed.

In their work with adolescents who stutter, Bray and Kehle (1996) suggested that highlighting "exemplary behaviors" contributes significantly to a reduction in stuttering. When participants in their study were shown three different five-minute video tapes of themselves *not* stuttering, and were encouraged to model these past exceptional moments, "all students' stuttering decreased in school and in various nonacademic settings" (p. 364). Visual and auditory reminders of times when the current problem was not a problem, and being coached to model their own non-problem behavior, appeared to facilitate a reduction in stuttering for these subjects.

Four types of exceptions have been proposed in the solution-focused literature (Nunnally, 1993). "Past exceptions" refer to experiences or occurrences in the student's past when the current presenting problem did not exist or was not recognized, such as not stuttering. "New exceptions" are non-problem instances that have only recently begun to happen, such as Mark refusing an offer to smoke marijuana with friends he used to hang out with. "Recurrent exceptions" are those instances that occur periodically in the present, often without warning and in an unpredictable fashion. An example of this would be the times Sherry is able to hit the C note she's struggled to get on her clarinet while marching in the band during a home game. "Future exceptions" refer to times in the future when the reported complaint will be eliminated or substantially reduced. The most popular solution-focused counseling technique, "The Miracle Question," is an attempt to formulate such future exceptions.

A distinctive quality of solution-focused school counselors is the ability to maintain a genuine inquisitiveness about their students in the midst of hectic days and student apathy. In the same manner, solution-focused school counselors intentionally and, over time, instinctively look for exceptions to problems, despite overwhelming evidence to the contrary. Drug sweeps, hallway fights, pregnant middle school students, budget cuts, custody battles, and so on can cloud or even erode our ability to see any light at the end of the tunnel for our students, our school, or ourselves. That is why it is imperative to train our mind's eye to detect even the subtlest variances in problem occurrences during the day, noticing the differences that de Shazer (1991) and Nelson (1998) have described. Remembering why you wanted to be a teacher or a school counselor in the first place may represent a past exception or difference to assist you in getting through an unusually difficult day at school.

Durrant (1995) has observed that "problems are what get people stuck, and a focus on these may lead to more stuckness" (p. 21). Therefore, noticing even minute and positive changes in the "same old, same old" events is the beginning of solution-formation and represents a hopeful and forward-looking direction.

The Miracle Question

Nuances of future-oriented and imaginal questions have been a part of therapeutic work for many years, especially with children. Play therapy is infused with "pretend" questions and scenarios in which children are encouraged to imagine a make-believe time that is better than the one they are currently experiencing.

Solution-focused practitioners, however, are credited with standardizing such an approach with clients of all ages who present a variety of initial complaints. Initially referred to as the "Crystal Ball Technique," and based on the work of Milton Erickson, it later was adapted by de Shazer (1985) as a tool intended to identify and visualize, and potentially make real, future exceptional periods. The Miracle Question, a form of future exceptions, is "designed to encourage clients to project themselves into a future situation in which the problem [is] no longer present, helping them to view themselves as functioning satisfactorily" (Molnar & de Shazer, 1987, p. 350). The question has since evolved into a specifically worded therapeutic strategy in which clients are challenged to imagine the resolution of the current problem the next morning:

> "Suppose that tonight, while you are asleep, there is a miracle and the problem that brought you into counseling today has been solved. However, because you are asleep you don't know that the miracle has already happened. When you wake up in the morning, what will be different that will tell you that this miracle has taken place?"

Children may describe their miracle as exactly that—a miracle! "Mommy and daddy would be married again to each other," "Gary would move far away so that he'd never call me names again," or "I'd be rich and wouldn't have to go to school." It is important that we not correct or discourage such responses from our students but, rather, encourage them to say more, so that we engage them in conversation. Keep in mind that the miracle question is intended to "help the client construct and consider a future without the problem" (Santa Rita, 1998, p. 189). Asking the question elicits a student's idiosyncratic and vivid description of a non-problem time. Therefore, there are no "right" or "wrong" answers!

Several authors have provided excellent suggestions for how to work with a client's response to the Miracle Question (Berg, 1994; Kral & Kowalski, 1989; Quick, 1996; Santa Rita, 1998). Follow-up questions to the responses cited above could include:

- "Tell me what that would be like for you, for your mommy and daddy to be married again to each other. How would it be different from when they were married to each other before? What would have changed? What would it be like for your mommy? What would it be like for your daddy?"
- "I can see, Kyle, that you really want your mommy and daddy to be married again to each other. It sounds like if they were back together again this would tell you that your miracle had really happened. This is a really big miracle, Kyle. Maybe a little too big for right now. Let's say you were only able to have a small piece of that

miracle for right now, what would that small piece be that would tell you that things were a little better for you than they are today?"

- "How would school be different for you if Gary had moved far away? What would change? How would you be different in your miracle than you are now? What would you be doing (or feeling) instead that you're not doing (or feeling) now? What else?"
- "So, you'd be rich and not coming to school. How would you know, when you woke up tomorrow morning that a miracle had actually happened during the night, while you were sleeping, and the miracle was that you were rich? How would you know you were rich? What would be different? Tell me what you'd be doing during the day instead of coming to school."

The Miracle Question is intended to further understand aspects of solutions that may already be occurring. Santa Rita (1998) suggested that by assisting clients to concretize or simplify their responses to the Miracle Question that clients can be challenged to "focus on the present, where solutions may exist, rather than on the uncertain future" (p. 190). He stated that sometimes clients can describe miracles that are rather ambitious or complex (such as Kyle's miracle that his parents would get married again to each other). In these instances Santa Rita recommended having clients break down the miracle into smaller parts and then asking clients to identify and select a piece of the miracle that would indicate to them that their current difficulties were in the process of being resolved. An example of this would be Kyle's description of a time when his mother and father wouldn't yell at each other when his father came to pick Kyle up for the weekend.

A modification of the Miracle Question is the "dream question" described by Greene, Lee, Mentzer, Pinnell, and Niles (1998). (The wording of the question here has been altered for its use with children and young teenagers.)

> "Suppose that tonight while you are sleeping you have a dream. In this dream you discover something inside yourself that you need to solve the problem that you are concerned about right now. When you wake up tomorrow, you may or may not remember your dream, but you do notice that you are different in some way. As you go about starting your day tomorrow, how will you know that you discovered something inside yourself necessary to solve your problem? What will be the first small bit of evidence that you did this?"

Greene et al. (1998) stated that the response to the "traditional" Miracle Question described by clients may be construed as the source of client change rather than something generated from the client. "Things happening in one's life due to 'luck,' 'accidents,' and 'chance' appear to be in the same class of phenomena as a 'miracle' in that their source is external to them and their own efforts" (p. 397). The dream question, on the other hand, conveys to clients and students that the solutions they are seeking can be discovered within themselves; that is, that they are the source of their solutions, not the miracle itself. Using the dream question in this manner, they argued, contributes to client (or student) empowerment.

The Miracle Question is not intended to make miracles happen—as if we had that capacity. Rather, asking the Miracle Question introduces students to and invites practice in new and different ways of thinking and doing. It challenges students to visualize or practice a time in the future that is removed from the present difficult, sad, or chaotic time they are experiencing. Chang (1998) mentioned that he finds it useful to encourage children to draw or to act out the miracle scene, rather than just talk about it. The visual portrayal or rehearsal of the miracle event "helps children enrich their descriptions of what the solution will look like" (p. 262). Thus, in describing and experiencing "in-the-moment" a future miracle time, students can be helped to identify things that are taking place right now in their lives that can contribute to a part of that miracle.

Divorced parents may not marry each other again, but their young child may realize that this is manageable, and may, in fact, not be such a bad thing, especially if unhappiness was pervasive before the separation. A school bully may not miraculously move far away overnight, but the student who has been teased may find ways to avoid or stand up to the teasing as the non-problem time is talked about. And being rich and not going to school may not be all that it's cut out to be, the more the student is encouraged to imagine it.

Although attention has been given in the solution-focused literature and in practice to asking the Miracle Question in a circumscribed fashion, Quick (1996) has suggested alternative wording, such as using "imagine," "pretend," or "let's say" to begin the question. With young children, the school counselor may want to introduce the concept of a "magic wand," suggesting that a pen or pencil could make a miracle happen right now (in the presence of the student), by waving the wand two or three times. If a student responds to the Miracle Question with shrugged shoulders or an "I don't know," Quick recommended that the counselor counter with, "If you had to guess, what would it be?" or, "Well, give it your best shot."

The value of the Miracle Question is in its ability to elicit a vivid and unique visualization of a non-problem future time. Solution-focused counselors would rather spend more time talking about the features of positive exceptions to the current problem than lingering on the details of a given complaint. As client and counselor talk further about the specifics of these non-problem miracles or dreams, strategies are cultivated and formed for how to make such "miracles" a present reality.

The Great "Instead"

In our attempts to identify past exceptional evidence in the student's life, or to help construct yet-to-be-realized "miracle moments," we are interested in visualizing and naming that which is different from the current issue or complaint. One way to elicit and emphasize this difference is to use the word "instead."

- "What could you do *instead* of running away?"
- "Okay, Aimee, let's say you don't mouth back at Ms. Potter the next time she tells you to be quiet in class. What would you do *instead*?"
- "Pretend that on Monday you're not as upset about Matt breaking up with you as you are now. What would you be thinking *instead* of 'how could he?' What else would you be doing *instead* of writing him notes and calling all his friends?"
- "How did you manage to get a 'B' in calculus *instead* of the 'D' you thought for sure you'd get? What did you do differently this time?"
- "What did you do *instead* of crying?"

The word "instead" is one to which most youngsters can relate, the meaning of which they can easily understand. It represents a substitute or alternative to problem behavior, something to be considered in place of a difficulty. The intentional inclusion of this word in our questions to students introduces them to the possibility that there are other ways to think, feel, and behave, other than what they are experiencing now. It challenges them to see situations and their place in them from another perspective.

Specific, Concrete, and Measurable Goals

A key feature of all brief or short-term counseling approaches is beginning with and keeping the goal of the student-counselor interaction in mind. This illustrates the goal-directed and goal-driven principle mentioned in chapter 1. Goal formulation establishes and maintains a focus for counseling, which is an essential component of brief therapy

(Cooper, 1995). Staying focused and, more specifically, always working toward the goal of counseling keeps both student and counselor on task and on track, not wasting a single minute. Such a focus increases the likelihood that the desired or appropriate outcome will be attained. Wandering, muddled, or confusing conversations are minimized; intentional and purposeful interactions are maximized.

A useful method to maintain focus and intentionality is to introduce and use the analogy that counseling is a road trip with a specific destination in mind. A road map or plan is needed to know how to get from one point to another and specific counseling tasks or strategies (the method of transportation, routes to take, road signs to watch for) are the means of finally arriving there.

> "Okay, gang. So that we don't end up wasting our time here, let's figure out where we need to go with this group. What's going to be our final destination seven weeks from now so that each of you feels that coming here in the afternoons was worth your time? When we get to that point, how will we know? What will the road signs tell us?"

> "We've been talking for a while, Sam. Where, exactly, are you headed with this? Where do you want to get to by having come in and talked with me today?"

> "What's the best map to use for getting to the point to where you will talk to your dad? Will you take a leisurely stroll about it, or get on a jet ski? When do you want to do this, and how, exactly, are you going to get to that point?"

Clarifying the destination of counseling, and doing so in specific and concrete terms, increases client-counselor cooperation and accelerates the process of change (Metcalf, 1995; Murphy, 1997). Precise, behaviorally specific, observable, and measurable descriptions of the goal are better than foggy or vague generalities: They can be manipulated, thereby increasing the likelihood of positive change. Compare the following goal descriptions:

Vague: *"I don't want to be sad all the time."*
Specific: *"I will be able to tell my teacher before I leave school one good thing I've learned each day."*

Vague: *"I want to get on with my life."*
Specific: *"I will finish the rest of my community service hours and drop off two job applications in the next two weeks."*

Vague: *"I wish I had more friends."*
Specific: *"I will raise my hand in class at least once a day and I will sit next to Arlene at lunch once this week."*

Vague: *"I just want my dad to be a real father."*
Specific: *"I will tell my dad straight-up but calmly tonight that the most important thing for me right now is for him to come to the tournament this weekend."*

Notice the obscure and noncommittal language of the vague goals and the clear, detailed, behaviorally specific, and certain ("I will") language used in the specific goals. The specific goals clarify when and what kind of new behavior will be implemented, as well as its frequency (e.g., "once a day"). They also specify the presence of something positive, rather than the absence of something negative (i.e., doing something other than just not "being sad all the time"). Movement and the assessment of such progress are therefore possible with specific goals (Berg & Miller, 1992a); uncertainty, idling, stuckness, and going around in circles are all perpetuated with vague goals.

Further Goal Formulations

Specificity and concreteness are only two aspects of well-constructed goals in solution-focused counseling. Other aspects are discussed throughout this chapter. The entire list of characteristics of well-constructed goals is found in Table 1.4 of chapter 1. Some of the features warrant discussion here.

The outcome of counseling needs to be determined jointly by counselor and student. Students, just as much as adults, need to have a voice in what the goal of counselor interactions will be. Ultimately, they will be the ones to determine whether or not working with the school counselor has been helpful. Goals, therefore, need to be constructed in a collaborative fashion, not prescribed or dictated by the counselor. In addition, goals need to be fashioned in a manner acceptable to the student, and in language he or she can understand. Sklare (1997) clarified that "obviously, ethical counselors do not support harmful goals" (p. 25).

In order for a student to accept and participate in a particular goal, it needs to be described as realistic, attainable, and within reach. Nick, the horticulture student described earlier in this chapter, would more than likely not buy into a goal of confronting the two female students who have been teasing him in science class the very next day. This task would be too great for him to accomplish at this time. Goals and their corresponding objectives, therefore, need to be framed in the here-and-now and tailored to the individual student (i.e., matching their motivational level and abilities). Furthermore, when described in a developmental or process form, rather than in a static or final form, students are more likely to become willing participants in the change process.

While goals need to be constructed as realistic, attainable, and within the student's reach, they also need to be perceived as requiring a certain amount of hard work (Berg & Miller, 1992a). Suggesting to Natalie that she just ignore questions from classmates about her recent discharge from a 90-day alcohol rehabilitation program minimizes the difficulty she faces getting back into the school environment. It also implies that Natalie won't be able to handle such questions. If Natalie's goal is to remain inconspicuous and not call attention to herself, she will need to understand that this will not be easy, that the transition back into school life will be a challenge, requiring, at times, considerable effort on her part. Failing to remain inconspicuous can then be attributed to the difficulty of the task, rather than a weakness in her.

Tipping the Domino

Getting the ball rolling toward the intended goal may involve a small step rather than a giant leap. Having the student tell the teacher one good thing learned in school at the end of each day may not solve a student's feeling of perpetual sadness. Such action, however, may tip the first domino and create what is known in solution-focused counseling as the "ripple" or "snowball" effect. One slight, baby step in the direction of change may instigate further, unpredicted, serendipitous movement toward a positive outcome.

The principle of parsimony mentioned in chapter 1 encompasses the notion of a ripple or snowball effect, and represents a feature of a well-constructed goal. A recommended formula is to suggest a simple, concrete, and achievable task to students first, before considering any in-depth, extended, and detailed plan of action. Telling dad forthrightly that his presence at the tournament this weekend is the most important thing right now may be all that it takes for the student to feel like his dad is trying to be a "real father." Family consultation or ongoing therapy may not be necessary. Students are more inclined to buy into the least-intrusive, least-restrictive, and least-threatening form of action than they are to sign their names to a lengthy, complicated, and time-consuming treatment plan.

Identifying a simple exception to a current problem and recommending that the student do more of it may facilitate a domino-type form of change. Bray and Kehle (1996) suggested this in their work with children who stutter. They proposed that self-modeling of non-stuttering times represents "the least restrictive, least intrusive, short-term, and effective intervention for the modification of stuttering" (p. 367). Identifying and practicing an exceptional behavior may be all that it takes to get the ball rolling!

Scaling Questions

Scaling and percentage questions are used frequently in solution-focused counseling to specify and better understand a client's feelings and aspirations, as well as to determine progress made.

- "On a scale of 1 to 10, 1 being completely petrified, and 10 being as confident as you could possibly be, where on this scale would you say you are now (or would like to be) about the try outs?"
- "What percent of the time do you feel like giving up? 25%? 50%? 75%? How does this compare to two months ago?"

Miller (1997) has referred to such questions as "the work horses of solution-focused therapy because they are frequently asked . . . to achieve a variety of therapeutic ends" (p. 12). Scaling and percentage questions are valuable because they:

1. quantify feelings, attitudes (e.g., confidence), motivations, and thoughts so that both the counselor and client understand where the client is and if they are on the same page; this serves to minimize misunderstandings
2. allow both the client and counselor to better conceptualize the client's present context and perspective
3. help the client express previously unexplainable feelings, attitudes, and so on; numerical answers help the client verbalize things that are hard for him or her to put into words
4. help clarify for both the client and counselor the goals of counseling, as well as defining what the next steps are (or should be) in arriving at that goal
5. assess how much progress has been made in the counseling interaction so far; client responses, then, serve as an "outcome measure," and help determine how much more work needs to be done in order for counseling to be complete at this time
6. focus on achievement and solutions
7. help instill a sense of change and progress; that is, by either moving "up" or "down" the scale, students can become aware that initial problems and symptoms are subsiding and desired feelings or behavior have increased in frequency or intensity

8. foster a sense in clients that they have some control in moving up or down scale, and that doing so is up to them
9. are used to assess variables involving relationships; for example, clients can be asked how other persons (e.g., parent, sibling, friend, teacher, etc.) would answer the same scaling question so that comparisons can be made

School counselors are encouraged to be creative with their use of scaling and percentage questions, so that they make sense to the student. Berg (1994) and Chang (1998) have described alternative and creative ways of asking, constructing, and visualizing scaling questions that solution-focused counselors who work primarily with children have reported using. With young children, a yardstick or a life-size thermometer (100 degrees equals "very, very mad" and 0 degrees equals "calm" or "not mad at all") as presented in Figure 4.1 can be used to provide possible incremental responses. Younger elementary students may relate better to a series of caricatured faces such as shown in Figure 4.2, colors, or other types of symbols that represent various feelings or behaviors (such as rain for sadness and the sun for happiness) more than can be represented on a numerical scale. When using nonnumerical symbols, however, it is best to present them in a linear

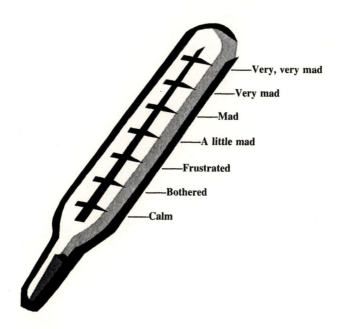

FIGURE 4.1. Incremental response scale: thermometer.

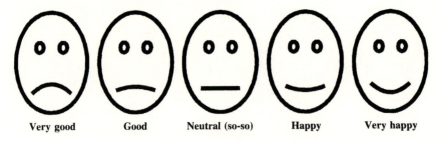

Very good   Good   Neutral (so-so)   Happy   Very happy

FIGURE 4.2. Incremental response scale: faces.

fashion (i.e., rather than in rows or columns, or in a circle, like a pie chart). Placing them in a line (and in equal increments) makes it possible to determine movement or progress.

Any time scaling or percentage questions are used it is important to qualify what the end points are on the scale (what the symbols stand for), so that students know how to judge the in-between points. Franklin et al. (1997) have recommended using self-anchored scales, which refer to allowing the client or the student to select what the anchors or the end points on the scale stand for (e.g., "fighting with my mom" vs. "getting along better with my mom"). Such scales, then, can represent and visualize the goal or outcome of the counseling encounter. When using scaling questions it is helpful to ask the same question at different times in the conversation (a "pretest" and a "posttest") or each time you meet with the student, so that both you and the student can keep track of his or her movement toward the stated goal or progress.

Two More Types of Questions

Solution-focused counselors are well known for asking many questions. The use of a variety of questions has been suggested as the "primary means of facilitating client change" (Greene et al., 1998, p. 396). The inquisitive and engaging nature of this approach suggests a preponderance of queries. Intentional questions will help shape solutions.

The questions, however, are not necessarily intended to simply gather additional information from clients, such as at an interrogation or a deposition. Rather, questions are posed as a means of clarifying complaints and solutions and, more importantly, eliciting client participation in the collaborative process of constructing solutions.

Coping Questions

Coping questions are designed to access elements of resilience or stamina that can be put to use to help a student get through challenging circumstances. Miller (1997) referred to these as "getting by" questions. They can be concerned with past accomplishments or can assist the student in devising a plan for a current or future hurdle. "How did you do that?" or "How did you ever manage that?" are examples of coping questions intended to identify the ingredients of past successes. "What would it take for you to do that?" encourages the student to identify specific tasks needed to get through and successfully manage impending challenges.

Imbedded in coping or getting by questions is a tone of commendation. Students can be commended or praised for past or recent efforts toward change by prefacing the question with "I'm amazed" or "I'm proud of you." Mark, a student with a history of aggressive behavior, was commended by his counselor for recently walking away from a fight: "Mark, you *are* reMARKable, do you know that? The word 're-markable' was invented with you in mind. How did you manage to walk away this time? What exactly did you do that made it possible for you to walk away?"

Relationship Questions

Relationship questions concern the involvement of other people in the student's current circumstance or constructed solution.

> "If Coach Hayes were here right now, what would he say about what you did in the locker room after the game Friday night? What would his version be?"

> "If you had to guess, what reason would you say there is for your mom to tell me that she's concerned about you right now?"

> "How will Mr. Wright know when you're trying your hardest to do better in his class? What would he be seeing in you that would convince him that you are trying harder?"

> "What did you and I talk about today that made this not a waste of your time? If you had to say one thing about our talk, maybe something I said, that was helpful, what would that one thing be?"

Solution-focused counselors view change as a joint or collective endeavor, not a solo act. Complaints and their solutions often involve and impact several persons—family members, classmates, teachers, neighbors, and friends. Without their side of the story, their ideas and stipulations of what constitutes a successful talk with the counselor, and their support of efforts made toward positive change, the purpose and goals of counseling interactions can be confusing and vague.

A 34-year-old married man and father of three girls desperately wanted to stop drinking. He had been drinking alcohol regularly for the past 15 years and had recently starting drinking again after having achieved three consecutive weeks of sobriety. Asked by his counselor about his reasons for drinking again, the despondent client responded, "No one noticed anything different."

For solutions to make a positive difference, to "take" or to "stick," other people in the student's life need to notice the changes made. Solicit from parents, teachers, principals, and classmates what they would need to see in the student's behavior that would tell them the student is back on track and making progress. Enlist these persons who interact regularly with the student as "detectives for solutions." The following questions can be posed to other persons in the student's life in an effort to solicit their recognition and support of the student's efforts at positive change:

- "What is one sign, a small clue, that has taken place in the past week that tells you, Mr. Clark, that Alex is trying to make amends?"
- "What will need to happen to convince you that Teresa is not going behind your back?"
- "When will you know that Troy has done his best? What will tell you?"

Questions such as these give others a "heads up" that solutions are in the making. And always checking in with your students about their impact on others and how others have contributed (or failed to contribute) to attempts at change promotes and refines their change-oriented behaviors.

☐ Summary of Strategies

We have described specific solution-focused strategies for use in a school setting with individual students. We do not believe, however, that such strategies *make* a solution-focused counselor, or make counseling solution-focused. Rather, it is your conviction that solutions are possible and your respectful, collaborative, earnest, and "exceptionally mindful" posture with students that make you a solution-focused counselor and your work solution-focused.

Fish (1997) proposed that solution-focused counseling "can be understood as a philosophy of life which suggests ways of talking to clients rather than as an autonomous set of easily learned clinical techniques" (p. 270). Strategies and techniques, therefore, take a back seat to an ability to establish a respectful relationship with your students. They also are second string to your confidence in the strengths and resources students bring with them when they meet with you.

Strategies simply illustrate and bring expression to the solution-focused philosophy. Using them in a naïve or haphazard fashion, then, becomes solution-*forced*, rather than solution-focused counseling (Nylund & Corsiglia, 1994). Use the strategies presented here selectively and appropriately. Know their purpose ahead of time so as not to compromise the well-being of your students.

☐ Solution-Focused Applications in Group Settings

Keys, Bemak, and Lockhart (1998) suggested that "it is unrealistic to assume that direct counseling services would be the most efficient and effective use of a counselor's time" (p. 385). They proposed group counseling as an important counseling format, particularly with at-risk youth, given time restrictions and the size of a school counselor's student case load.

The solution-focused counseling approach is well suited for group counseling (Metcalf, 1998), particularly in a school setting (LaFountain, Garner, & Eliason, 1996). Its time sensitive and short-term model makes scheduling and time constraints more manageable. In addition, the emphasis on what students are already doing well makes it possible for group members to serve as positive role models for one another.

The solution-focused strategies described earlier in this chapter can be easily transferred and used in a group setting. Within a time-sensitive framework, the group will need to begin with a clearly stated purpose and objective, in language students can understand. Conforming to the criteria of well-constructed goals (see Table 1.4 in chapter 1), individual member and group goals should be described in positive, nonpathological terms, and presented as the presence of new behaviors, not merely the absence of the presenting problem.

It's All in the Name

One of the first places in which to implement these criteria is in the naming of the group. The name given to a particular counseling or psychoeducational group speaks volumes about its relevance, attraction to members, and thus the potential for group cohesiveness, and ability to promote positive change—and thus its goal. Naming a group by the problem shared among group members perpetuates a focus on what's wrong, rather than on possible solutions and positive outcomes. An "Anger Management Group" implies simply lassoing and containing problematic anger, as opposed to teaching and cultivating alternative, more positive and socially acceptable behaviors.

Just as mental health diagnoses can be misused in inappropriate, harmful, and demeaning ways, names applied to groups can be unfair to group members, furthering the stigma of being "sick" or "totally messed up." Who wants to acknowledge to classmates that he has to attend his "Conduct Disorder Group" during fifth period? And what attraction, let alone hope for feeling and doing better, is there in advertising and referring to a group as the "Loner's Club" or the "Substance Abusers Group"?

Name the group by its positive goal (e.g., "Friendship Club"), not its problem. This instills in members (and the leader!) right from the start that the group is about positive change, not about permanent problems. It also provides members with a clear and ever-present focus for group time. The name, "Stronger Every Day," for a group of students who have witnessed the death of a family member or friend to a violent crime, communicates its purpose: "We're here to work through and move beyond the crisis, not re-live it." Similarly, the name "Rising Stars" for a group offering tutoring and support for academically challenged sixth graders, implies that progress, achievement, and success are in store for members. Names such as these may also be ones that not only attract new members, but also one that members feel good about and are proud of, names for groups they wouldn't mind telling others they attend.

Encourage members to participate in the naming of the group, if a generic name exists. Group names should be generated from group goals, which should describe the presence of something positive, not just the elimination of something negative. An example is the "Trust" group for high school students who are recovering from substance abuse problems. Being able to contribute to the naming of a group helps build cohesiveness and challenges members to articulate exactly what they want to get out of the group.

Common Language

Participating in the naming of a solution-focused group is one way to introduce members to the principles of a solution-focused philosophy. Problems will need to be discussed and clarified, but they will not dominate collective discourse (Metcalf, 1998). Mention will be made of diminishing or eradicating problems, but what to do *instead* of problematic thinking and behaving will be the center of attention.

The leader plays an important role in educating members about the reality and intent of solution construction. He or she models the use of salutary or nonpathological language. The leader also challenges members to use more appropriate, interactive, and goal-oriented forms of expression, such as "I will" rather than "I can't." The leader must also point out and correct (when necessary) language conveys permanent stuckness or perpetual disaster.

As with most groups, members are encouraged to use "I" statements when communicating observations, opinions, and first person experiences. The use of such pronouns promotes genuine interaction and a sense of empowerment. Members can be encouraged to "catch" one another using nonpersonal pronouns, such as "you" or they," and gently assist their peers to restate the message in an "I" statement.

Co-Conspirators

In a solution-focused group, members act as "co-conspirators" in the development and identification of strengths, competencies, and other exceptions to problems in one another. The group leader is not the only "detective." Some students may be better able to detect positive attributes in another member before they can identify similar exceptions in themselves.

An appropriate group exercise is to place each group member "on assignment." The assignment is to secretly "catch" another group member saying or doing something positive right before, during, or after group time. Reports are then given at the close of each group session as a means of highlighting exceptions and commending group members for noticing positive differences in one another.

Members, then, can become increasingly aware of their own resources and abilities as they witness examples of strengths and resources in others (Metcalf, 1998). Furthermore, receiving a compliment or commendation from a peer often has a more powerful impact than one received from an adult, namely the school counselor and group leader, whose "job" it is to "help me feel better." Peers aren't obligated to point out the positive aspects observed in others, such as courage, sincerity, and helpfulness. In fact, doing so may often represent a risk: a risk of looking like the counselor's "pet," or being phony, or that one's simply flirting, or merely trying to align oneself with the "popular" group member. The solution-focused school counselor and group leader, however, is committed to noticing and articulating such commendations in his or her students.

Clearly Speaking

Solution-focused groups are action-oriented. This means that what takes place within the group is intended to facilitate positive movement and change among members. LaFountain et al. (1996) observed that "solution-focused counseling groups seem to provide a context for goal achievement" (p. 264).

As discussed in chapter 4, the use of presuppositional, scaling, and Miracle and other exception-finding questions can help to promote goal attainment. Clarifying the intended destination, goal, or outcome provides direction for individual members as well as for the entire group. Well-timed, appropriate, and relevant questions, therefore, from the group leader and from members, assist in identifying and clarifying where members are and where they want to be.

Scaling questions can be used in a round to open and close group sessions. "On a scale of 1 to 10, 1 being 'lousy' and 10 being 'on top of the world,' where would you say you are today?" can be used to open a group session. Responses assist in determining the focus for the session and clue other group members on the status of their peers. A similar question can be used to wrap up a session, such as, "On a scale of 1 to 10, 1 being 'not at all' and 10 being 'extremely, no doubt about it,' how helpful would you say this group has been for you today?" Members can be asked for more specifics regarding factors that contributed to the helpfulness or nonhelpfulness of the group session that day.

Summary of Solution-Focused Groups

For many students, the group setting can serve as an exception in itself. Members may not have an opportunity elsewhere to be listened to by their peers, to observe positive and healthy forms of communication, or to experience a glimmer of hope in their lives. Regardless of the ages of members or the purpose of the group, the leader assumes the responsibility for establishing and cultivating a confident atmosphere of positive change and improvement. In this manner the solution-focused group becomes an instrument of change in itself, rather than merely a collection of individuals.

CHAPTER

Working with Children of Challenge and Their Parents

One of the most challenging tasks that a school counselor faces is trying to gain the confidence and support of the parents of students with whom he or she work. This chapter will address considerations and recommendations for school counselors in their efforts to develop productive working relationships with parents and with difficult or challenging students. In doing so, the school counselor must consider many contextual issues that will impact their effectiveness.

☐ Working with Difficult Students

If counseling is about change, it is unreasonable to expect that all the students with whom you work want to change. "Difficult," "reluctant," "resistant," "in denial," and "unmotivated," or "apathetic" students can often be the rule rather than the exception for school counselors. Research indicates that a majority of adults presenting themselves for professional counseling are not aware that they need to change or are ambivalent about changing (Prochaska, DiClemente, & Norcross, 1992). Students are no different. Change is often a formidable and difficult task, and expecting students to be gung-ho about talking to you and working with you toward change is a naïve, unrealistic, and dangerous position from which to practice.

Difficulty Defined

What defines "difficult" deserves clarification. We find it helpful, particularly from a solution-focused perspective, to describe an *interaction* or *relationship* with a student as difficult, rather than a particular student. Berg and Miller (1992a) suggested a similar approach with problematic substance users. Resistance is more a characteristic of the counselor-client relationship than of the client and serves as a signal that the counselor and client are not in agreement about the goals or objectives of counseling (Miller & Rollnick, 1991).

Kottler (1997) suggested certain clues for recognizing a difficult interaction with a student or, in his words, knowing "when a student has gotten underneath your skin" (p. 28):

- when you spend an inordinate amount of time thinking about a particular child, or complaining about him or her to others;
- when you repeatedly find yourself misunderstanding a child and feeling misunderstood yourself by him or her;
- when you are aware of feeling particularly frustrated, helpless, and blocked with a child; and
- when your empathy and compassion are compromised and you find it difficult to feel respectful and caring toward a child.

Experiences such as these are not solely about the student; rather, they describe the *interaction* between counselor and student. When a counselor engages in consistent confrontation, the relationship will become resistant; when a counselor solicits cooperation from a student, resistance will be minimal (Miller et al., 1993; Miller & Sovereign, 1989; Patterson & Forgatch, 1985). How the counselor views and responds to the student contributes to the type of working relationship that is formed. Resistance, therefore, is a *counselor*, not a student, problem (Miller & Rollnick, 1991).

Lose the Label

Students are often referred to the school counselor with a label already attached to them. "Trouble maker," "AD/HD," "social outcast," "air head," "grunge," and "jock" are descriptions that precede some of the students with whom you meet—and they know it. Young persons are particularly vulnerable to such descriptions and will often live up to their label, using the adjective bestowed upon them to explain away their difficulties:

"What'd you expect from the 'liar' Mrs. Thomas says I am? That I'd come here and spill my guts out on the floor to you?"

"I've never really had any friends. I guess it's 'cause I've always had low self-esteem. My mom probably already told you that."

"I just snapped. I don't know what happened. I just got angry. I've always been angry—at least that's what everyone says about me."

If we as counselors aren't careful, we'll interact with students according to their label, allowing someone else's judgment or our first impressions to categorize the student and govern how we work with him or her.

A reliance on labels to describe people is dangerous for several reasons. Labels squelch a young person's positive self-image and serve as convenient excuses for problematic behavior. They are also vague and nondescript, providing little useful information relevant to who this particular student is and what he or she is thinking and experiencing in the present moment. "He's depressed" or "she's unmotivated" tell us relatively nothing about a particular student. More information is needed for such descriptions to have any value, such as how the depression is recognized by the teacher or experienced by the student, or in what ways the student seems to lack motivation. Asking specific and behavioral questions assists in obtaining information helpful to better conceptualize the student's experience of a perceived problem. Examples include:

"Tell me, exactly, what you think has given Mrs. Thomas reason to say that you're a 'liar'? How did she ever get that notion? Do you agree?"

"What exactly do you mean by 'low self-esteem,' Leslie? What tells you that you have what you call 'low self-esteem?' How do you know you have it?"

"Tell me what it's like for you to feel yourself starting to get angry, Nathan. How would I know if or when you were starting to feel angry? What would be the first sign for me? What would I see you doing? What might I hear you saying?"

In their work with adolescents, Biever, McKenzie, Wales-North, and Gonzalez (1995) and Selekman (1993) recommended working with the person, not the label. This requires an intentional effort on the counselor's part, especially with students who have a history of problems. Losing the label involves taking time to investigate the student's experience of and perspective on his or her circumstance. In learning more about the individual, sweeping generalizations disappear and distinctive qualities become more evident.

Deflating Difficulty

In addition to losing the label, Kottler (1997) and Osborn (1999) recommended additional strategies for working effectively with 'involuntary' clients or those who contribute to difficult counseling interactions.

Solicit Student's Story.   Offer ample opportunity for students to tell their side of the story. This may be a particularly difficult task when you are well-acquainted with the student's history of problem behavior. Allowing the student to express what he or she needs to say within certain parameters (e.g., one sentence, ten words or less, or within five minutes) about a particular issue communicates intentional interest and respect.

Acknowledge Aggravation.   Students who have been coerced into talking with the school counselor are going to display frustration. Acknowledge this and commiserate with the student's described circumstance. "I know you'd much rather be doing something else right now than sitting here talking to me. This may all seem to you like a big joke and a total waste of your time. But, hey, you're stuck with me for this period. We need to think of what needs to happen so that Mr. Kensington doesn't have any more reason to keep sending you down here to see me."

Investigate, Don't Interrogate.   This is where the "Curious Columbo" detective skills discussed in chapter 3 take center stage. Find out as much as you can about the context of the problem. When does it occur? Where does it occur? With whom does it occur? When does it *not* occur? Find out as much you can about the student's side of the story by assuming a stance of "not knowing."

Clarify, Don't Confront.   In attempts to clarify the issue at hand and identify potential solutions, be careful not to unfairly or unnecessarily challenge the student. Such confrontation discourages any willingness to participate and may cause the student to shut down. Prefacing sentences with "Help me understand . . ." and "I may be way out in left field on this one, so correct me if I'm wrong . . ." signal to the student an attempt to clarify issues in an egalitarian fashion.

Level, Don't Lecture.   Students need to understand the natural consequences of problematic behavior and alternatives available to them. Teenagers in particular appreciate clear or "straight up" communication rather than being fed a line. Leveling with a student implies genuine rather than contrived interaction, and dialogue rather than monologue.

Cooperate, Don't Convince.   Adopt a cautious and respectful attitude. Maintain a "one-down" position in which you present yourself in the role of consultant rather than authority figure. Ritchie (1994) referred to this as an invitation to the child to be your partner.

Collaborate with Collaterals.   Students meeting with you involuntarily have been sent by someone else (a teacher or parent) who has some interest in the outcome. It is important to involve such persons in your work with the student, especially if the student is not forthcoming with information or is unwilling to cooperate. Asking Ken's mom what specifically will convince her that Ken is doing his best in school provides you and Ken with a goal to work toward. Checking in with Ken's mom over the course of your work with him and asking what she's noticed differently in his behavior alerts her to the inevitability of change.

Solicit Solutions, Don't Prescribe Them.   Students who are part of difficult issues or situations are often simply stuck. They do not see other alternatives that work as well as what they are already doing. Remember that students have the resources to solve the given problem. They may simply need a measure of support, encouragement, and guidance to resolve things to everyone's satisfaction.

Commend, Don't Condemn.   Attempting to uncover the reasons behind a student's circumstance is often a futile endeavor. Causal explanations do not contribute to solution construction. It is important, therefore, to move beyond blame and assigning guilt. Find reason to commend a student for staying on track or at the very least not making things worse.

☐ Parents as Partners in Building Solutions

Counselors are often faced with uncooperative parents, not willing to take an active role in their child's education. Chang (1998) has suggested that the majority of parents perceive the problem as residing in their child, rather than as a manifestation of family relationships or the family system. The problem, therefore, can be construed by a parent as being "out of my hands" and for someone else to "fix." By the same token, parents are often frustrated with a school system that they believe sees their child as a number within the system, unwilling to try to understand the unique qualities and challenges facing their sons or daughters.

Parents can indeed be introduced to a solution-focused perspective that will allow them to interface with the school more effectively. In turn, parenting can be approached from a solution-focused point of view, giving parents specific ways of thinking which can enhance their relationships with their children.

It is important to keep in mind the notion that being solution focused is much more than a means to approach problems within a school context; it is a way of thinking, and a process of addressing people and the problems that they face (Murphy, 1997). As the school counselor begins to infuse a solution-focused philosophy within the school context, a natural progression would be to expand the concepts outside the doors of the school into the homes of parents and children with whom the counselor works.

Diversity and the School Counselor

As the school counselor begins to look for ways to partner with the parent in supporting and facilitating the personal, social, and educational growth of the student, there are many critical aspects connected with the family that must be considered. We must understand that our schools are made up of students who come from a wide range of cultural and racial backgrounds. When counselors understand the cultural backgrounds of the students whom they serve they will be in a position to forge much stronger working relationships, built on respect, and trust.

In his book *Counseling for Diversity: A Guide for School Counselors and Related Professionals,* Courtland Lee (1996) puts forward seven racial and ethnic variations in the cultural context of families that are critical to the school counselor in forging a meaningful working relationship with the family members.

Notions of Kinship. There appear to be important cultural differences in the emphasis placed on bonds of interpersonal affiliation established within family and community kinship networks. In some cultural traditions, a major emphasis is placed on the nuclear family and individual autonomy. In others, great importance is placed on extended family kinship networks and interdependence among individuals. This individual versus communal distinction in kinship social organization can affect the development of perceptions and attitudes regarding relationships with individuals, social groups, and institutions among young people.

Roles and Status.   Cultural differences exist with respect to roles and status within families and communities. Central to this are prescribed notions or traditions concerning individual responsibilities and obligations that are based on age- and gender-defined roles and status. Children and adolescents are socialized into roles and assigned status within a family and community hierarchy based on such notions.

Sex-Role Socialization.   There are cultural differences concerning perceptions of the role of males and females. Differential gender perceptions can influence the expectations considered normal for psychosocial development. Such expectations may account for fundamental differences in personality development for boys and girls in the traditions of many cultures.

Language.   Acquisition and use of language is an important aspect of socialization for young people. Mastery of language often fosters success in future developmental tasks. Children are socialized into a language tradition at an early age. There are, however, significant cultural differences in language traditions, as well as the value placed on specific language use. Personality development in childhood and adolescence can be significantly affected by distinctions in language traditions. This is particularly evident when there is a conflict of cultural perceptions regarding differences in language traditions and values.

Religion/Spirituality.   Religious and spiritual influences are universally important in shaping the formation of behavior and values in young people. However, there are significant cultural differences in the extent to which such influences may affect childhood and adolescent psychosocial development. The distinctions between religious and secular life vary across cultural groups. The degree of such distinctions among families and communities can significantly affect aspects of personality development.

Ethnic Identity.   Dynamics such as those just given, when considered in their totality, contribute greatly to the development of an ethnic identity among young people. Ethnic identity is the primary principle for understanding psychosocial development in a cultural context. It can be considered as the inner vision that one develops of oneself as an African American, Arab American, Korean American,

Mexican American, Native American, or Italian American. Ethnic identity greatly influences psychosocial development, particularly in a culturally pluralistic country such as the United States.

Lee (1995) has put forward these critical factors related to diversity to which the school counselor must attend if there is any hope of working effectively with the family. The context from which the student comes will have a great influence on the ability of the school counselor to gain the trust of the student, parents, or guardian. It will also greatly influence the potential effectiveness of the school counselor's interventions.

It is important that school counselors adopt a pluralistic view of society. School counselors must understand cultural differences relative to the students who are served by their own school districts. Having an appreciation and understanding of people from different backgrounds allows the counselor to appreciate thoughts, behaviors, and feelings of both students and family members being served.

Solution-focused counseling has been shown to be effective with a broad cultural population (Berg & Miller, 1992b; De Jong & Berg, 1998; DeJong & Hopwood, 1996). In addition, studies point out that because the solution-focused approach draws upon client perceptions and works more fully within their frames of reference, this approach is effective across diverse groups. It is important that counselors be aware of the need for understanding diverse populations. The client's perceptions are shaped by their histories, customs, and problem-solving styles of their culture, and solution building integrates those aspects of diversity as it proceeds.

☐ Solution-Focused Parent Conferences

A constant theme heard from school personnel is that there is a need for greater parental involvement for the improvement of student performance. We know that there seems to be greater success from those students whose parents take an active role in their educational development.

Often, a parent's first personal communication with a school official is when their child has had some sort of problem at school. This often lays the groundwork for conflict between the parent and school officials. The school counselor taking a solution-focused approach would act differently with parents. As Murphy (1997) has suggested, the school must certainly address those situations where a student has violated school policy by calling in the parents or guardians. However, the school counselor using a solution-focused approach would be looking for those situations when things are going right; particularly in situations where a student is in trouble with the school, the school counselor would contact the parents to notify them when things are going well. The counselor would want to ask the parent questions such as "What is currently happening that is different from when the problem was occurring?" or "Have you noticed a change at home for the better, and what is being done differently from before?"

Taking such an approach with the entire student body is not realistic given all of the demands that school counselors find themselves dealing with today. The school counselor can, however, employ this approach with the parents whose children have run into trouble at school.

In addition, the school counselor might also use such an approach with those students who might be considered "at risk." This is an approach that allows the school counselor to communicate with the parent about situations concerning their children that are of a positive nature.

Guidelines for Planning
a Parent-Teacher Conference

In her book *Parenting Towards Solutions*, Linda Metcalf (1997) makes recommendations to parents who are about to attend a parent-teacher conference. Parents should be proactive by requesting a parent-teacher conference before serious problems arise. Parents should take an active role in the meeting by framing the conversation around a "win-win" philosophy. Metcalf points out that in such conferences parents might find their child being compared and evaluated against other students, making it a "win-lose" proposition. Metcalf submits an eight step solution-focused approach to such a conference. She recommends that parents might consider the following steps:

1. Ask for an administrator or school counselor to be present (particularly when there has been some form of conflict).
2. Ask for everyone's version of the problem.
3. Ask for everyone's exceptions to the problem. (This allows for maximum views and potential alternatives and exceptions to the problem.)
4. Compile a list of the exceptions from everyone involved in the meeting. It is critical that all involved are aware that there are exceptions to the problem and that these will be valuable to all involved. Tell your child to show the teachers something different for just a

week and that the teachers will be watching. Ask your child to tell everyone what would be helpful for him or her.

5. Tell your child to show the teachers something different for a specified period of time (such as a week). Ask your child to notice those things that the teachers are doing that seems to be helpful.

6. Suggest to the teachers to offer your child feedback concerning those times when your child is doing better.

7. Be certain to acknowledge those teachers who do things differently and encourage your child's success.

The school counselor can actively seek to encouragde parents to take an active role in the parent teacher conference. Parents may feel empowered by being active in their child's education and may be encouraged to adopt a "parenting towards solutions" way of thinking.

☐ Solution-Focused Parenting Groups

School counselors can be very helpful in helping parents develop better communication skills, which in turn, can facilitate better relationships with their children. Parents typically fall into regimented patterns of behavior relative to their communication styles. Parents often employ patterns that they have modeled from their parents or other grown-ups when they were children. Such patterns, if negative in nature, can be troublesome to the parent-child relationship, and will at best yield limited desired results. The school counselor can offer many positive parenting alternative approaches. Specifically, the school counselors can teach solution-focused concepts to parents to enhance their parenting skills.

Selekman (1991) put forward a recommendation for a six session solution-oriented parenting group. The groups are built around seven core assumptions which serve as principles that govern the groups. They are:

1. *Change is inevitable.* One thing for certain is that we are all constantly changing. It is important for parents to understand that because change will always occur, there will always be opportunities to have a positive impact on that change.

2. *Only a small change is necessary.* This is an important assumption for the parent to acquire. People want so badly to have problems solved immediately and completely. In reality, minor changes will create more exceptions to the problems and an opportunity to consider exceptions to when the problem is occurring.

3. *Parents and adolescents have the strengths and resources to change.* Parents must first have faith that all individuals have the capacity to change for the better.
4. *If it works, don't fix it.* Parents must be able to see through he problem and recognize those things that are working. Once those things that are working have been identified, parents are encouraged not to tinker with them.
5. *If it doesn't work, do something different.* This may be the most difficult thing of all to address. Parents can have a tendency to go back to the old behaviors time and time again, with no evidence that "this time, it will be different."
6. *No problem happens all of the time.* There are always times when the problem is not occurring. The task of the parent is to be able to identify those times when it is not happening.
7. *There are many ways to look at a situation, none of which is more "correct" than the another.* Parents benefit themselves by considering multiple alternatives to a problem. There can indeed be many correct ways to see that the problem is addressed.

Selekman (1991) suggests that the process of change is a constant phenomenon. Families are in a constant state of evolutionary flux. He goes on to suggest that from the beginning of the first parenting group session the counselor should try to convey the idea to parents that change is only a matter of "when" it "will" happen with their children. This is a very powerful perspective. By expecting change to occur, it will in turn influence their children.

The parenting group presented here consisted of parents with chemically dependent children (Selekman, 1991). It should be stressed, however, that this approach to training parents is appropriate for any challenges facing the student. Groups may be run for parents using these methods to assist their children with study skills, relationship development, career decision making, or any other topic for that matter. Selekman offered the following six session model:

Session #1: Solution-Oriented Parenting: A New Way of Thinking and Doing.   The introductory session includes a time for introductions, including inquiry into parents' work, hobbies, and interests, to help determine strengths that the parents might bring to their relationship with their children. In addition, the counselor should address the core assumptions of solution-oriented parenting, which will give the parents a foundation for the group sessions to follow. A homework assignment is given to the parents in the form of an observational request. They are asked to write down all of the positive behaviors that they observe their child engaging in over the next week.

Session #2: Going for Small Changes.   This group begins with the counselor requesting each parent to report all positive changes that they observed with their child. The counselor should reinforce the point that change is always happening. In addition, parents are asked to consider what they are doing when their child's problem isn't there. The parent might say something like "I'm talking in a calm manner, not yelling or nagging."

The use of scaling questions is introduced to reinforce the importance of understanding degrees of change. This, in turn, leads to what might have to happen to improve on the scale. This is considered goal setting. Discussion focuses upon the necessity of establishing realistic, achievable goals.

Session #3: If It Works, Don't Fix It.   The parents are encouraged to look for what works. What is happening when the child is engaged in desirable behavior? Parents can be so consumed with the anticipation of something bad happening, that they can tend to look right past those times when the negative behavior is *not* occurring. The focus of this session is to determine what steps were achieved towards the attainment of their goal (e.g., "I will continue to remain composed when my child talks back to me. Overreacting only makes the problem worse.").

Session #4: If It Doesn't Work, Do Something Different.   Changing well-ingrained responses can be one of the most difficult things that a parent must do. It is so easy for parents to continually use disciplinary measures that have worked with some degree of success early on, but yield little or no positive returns as time has passed. Working with parents to learn new and creative parenting strategies is critical in this session. Parents can learn to generate new responses to old, negative behaviors. Helping parents learn that experiencing alternatives to old reactions to their children's negative behavior offers hope for finding solutions.

Session #5: Keeping Change Happening.   Selekman (1991) suggested that this session be used as a time to explore the ingenuity of the participants. Pooling the creative strategies of the participants helps to vividly demonstrate the power of the parents to abandon their old ineffective approaches, and instead, employ more effective techniques.

It is important that the counselor infuse the session with encouragement and praise for positive change. Offering compliments or commendations to the group members and being a cheerleader for their efforts will be reinforcing, and at the same time will serve as a model for the group members who will in turn offer support for each other.

Session #6: Celebrating Change.   The final session is used to recap the elements that contribute to solution-oriented parenting. Parents should have an opportunity to highlight those things that have happened that will let other people know that there is movement towards solutions in their relationship with their children. It will be important that the counselor offer clinically sound recommendations in those cases where goal attainment has not been reached, depending upon the type of focus group, such as substance abuse or relationship building. This could include referrals or other forms of intervention.

Such a group can be developed for parents who are struggling to find answers to problems that are being experienced by their children. Solution-oriented parenting groups can be a valuable intervention for the school counselor who is attempting to address student needs via the assistance of parents.

☐ Summary

Solution-focused counseling distinguishes among three different types of counseling relationships: (1) the customer type, (2) the complainant type, and (3) the visitor type (Berg & Miller, 1992a; de Shazer, 1988). The customer type relationship exists when goals have been identified jointly by the counselor and student, and students have the view that he or she is a part of the solution. The complainant relationship exists when a goal has been identified, but the student does not see that they are a part of the change process. In this instance, the student may understand and be in agreement with the counseling process, but does not believe that he or she is responsible for any of the changes. Lastly, the visitor type relationship lacks both a jointly constructed counseling goal and the student's participation in the change process.

Complainant and visitor counseling relationships are often experienced as frustrating and difficult. Berg and Miller (1992a), however, have encouraged counselors to look for the "hidden customer" in their work with clients and students. This implies that frustration and difficulty be viewed as initial and temporary kinks or side effects, rather than as permanent fixtures, with students who present challenging issues and circumstances. Furthermore, gearing the counseling interaction to the "hidden customer" implies that we look beyond or, perhaps more appropriately, *through* the frustrating and annoying distractions of a challenging student to the individual who is motivated to do or to be something, albeit a something that may conflict with the needs, standards, rules, requirements, or expectations of those around the student. If we are able to understand the motivations or intentions of a young person (including the problem-focused and thinking behavior as proposed by Dreikurs [1964] and as discussed in chapter 3), we then have a glimpse of a "hidden customer," that is, someone to whom we can tailor our services in a manner in which that person will cooperate, or at least hear us and consider the possibility of cooperating.

In her work with juvenile offenders, all of whom could be considered visitors or complainants, Corcoran (1997) has recommended a solution-oriented approach. The advantages are that it (1) highlights the present-focus typical of most adolescents; (2) downplays discussion of the past, problems, and feelings; and (3) utilizes the adolescent's short attention span by encouraging movement toward change in a brief period. If solution-focused counseling can be deemed an appropriate intervention with juvenile offenders, imagine its utility with *all* adolescents and children!

The rewards of school counseling can begin to outnumber its hassles when counselors are able to view their work as helping students manage difficulties, rather than fixing their problems, and assisting them to get back on track toward their goals, rather than "curing" their ailments once and for all. Solution-focused counseling offers such a perspective: It provides school counselors with reason for hope in the midst of hardship, and practical tools for working toward possible solutions.

CHAPTER

The Solution-Focused School

We have emphasized so far in the book the important role of the school counselor in solution-focused counseling. The school counselor is the primary purveyor of this nonpathological, competency-based approach in the school setting. Without active and deliberate detection and cultivation of exceptions to student problems, the process of constructing solutions is severely hampered and suffers.

Solution-focused school counseling, however, does not and cannot operate and thrive in a vacuum. We all know that positive and durable change is not possible unless we have the cooperation of parents, teachers, and school administrators. Working with parents from a solution-focused perspective was addressed in the chapter 5. This chapter will discuss "the bigger picture"; that is, the work of *all* school personnel in an effort to establish an "exceptional" solution-focused school.

☐ Don't Look at *Me*!

We have acknowledged throughout the book the enormous amount of responsibility and varied duties that school counselors are typically expected to carry out. We suspect that for many of you, your vision of school counseling before you became a school counselor does not match your current job description or your daily duties. How often do we see new mandates for student services coming to our schools, and the first professional approached to take on the new task is the school counselor?

Our instinctive reaction is often "Don't look at me!" Both Baker (1996) and Gysbers and Henderson (1994) listed a plethora of professional activities that many school counselors find themselves doing, duties that are ancillary or considered secondary to providing counseling, mental health, and other types of therapeutic services directly to students. Included in their lists are such things as:

- registering and scheduling all new students,
- administering ability and achievement tests,
- signing excuses for students who are tardy or absent,
- teaching classes when teachers are absent,
- being assigned to lunchroom duty,
- sending students home who are not appropriately dressed,
- assisting with duties in the principal's office, and
- secretarial and clerical tasks.

One reason Gysbers and Henderson (1994) offered for school counselors feeling overwhelmed by and confined in a multitude of diverse duties is that "some counselors are unwilling to see others playing a role in the delivery of the guidance program . . . [and] they feel that it is their job to carry out the total program" (p. 43). Anderson and Reiter (1995) added that their "instincts as helpers" (p. 268) and fears of increasing cutbacks contribute to school counselors accepting such "add-on" tasks. School counselors, therefore, may bear some responsibility in perpetuating their involvement in menial professional activities secondary to counseling duties.

The solution-focused school is possible only when other professionals outside the counseling staff are on board and actively involved. This requires the proactive and persistent outreach of school counselors to educate *all* school personnel about a solution-focused philosophy. The solution-focused school, therefore, begins with the school counselor as he or she challenges the traditional deficit model of operation and demonstrates the alternative competency-based approach to serving students.

This chapter offers a framework for conceptualizing and constructing a solution-focused school. Recommendations are provided for modeling the approach and enlisting cooperation from others.

☐ Focus on Principals

School counselors and school principals have been characterized as operating from different paradigms (Kaplan, 1995). Counselors value individual student interaction, view students' mental health as a valid end or goal for counseling, and tend to work within a process orientation. Principals, on the other hand, are more group or community centered, view students' mental health as a means to academic achievement, and tend to be more action-and-concrete-results oriented.

From a solution-focused perspective, *both* paradigms are valid and necessary. Changing the way we view our roles and functions can be difficult. There is a strong connection between what we do on a daily basis and what is reinforced by existing theory (Sergiovanni, 1994). Maintaining old ways becomes automatic and difficult to change, and familiar practices can become unquestionable truths.

Short and Greer (1997) suggested that when principals relinquish control and share it with teachers and others in the school, everyone experiences more responsibility for the quality of work that is produced. Trust-building leads to meeting the needs of all involved, a respect for diversity, and a willingness to seek solutions without the threat of reprisal.

Beale (1995) proposed that "the principal is the single most influential person when it comes to selecting school counselors" (p. 216). The solution-focused school, therefore, can only operate with the principal's full endorsement and active participation. Metcalf (1995) offered three guiding principles for principals that aid in supporting both teachers and students in solution-focused efforts.

Principals, first, must be *accepting*. Both teachers and students need to feel that they are in a place where they are wanted and needed. Accepting means that their thoughts and feelings are free to be aired to the principal. Second, teachers and students need to be *validated*. When a teacher says that Jane constantly acts out in class, that is exactly what the teacher believes. When Jane says that Ms. Jones is always on her back, that is exactly what the student believes. Neither view is the "right" or accurate one. Both Jane and Ms. Jones understandably feel frustrated, annoyed, or angry; these represent their experiences in the present moment, and these feelings need to be heard and validated.

Finally, Metcalf (1995) stated that both teachers and students need *structure*. When an individual begins to feel out of control, the most important stabilizing response is to have a structured protocol to follow. In the case of Jane and Ms. Jones, structure may represent allowing an opportunity for each to express her feelings, and then soliciting from each of them suggestions for what to do next. An additional stabilizing and structuring task may be to encourage each to describe what has been happening when the problem is not active.

All three principles represent a strategic plan for how the school principal can instill trust and cooperation in both teachers and students.

It is critical that we bring the school principal on board and as any CEO, enlist them to help carry the banner of transformation to a "solution-focused school."

☐ Imagine What Your School Will Be When . . .

A beneficial and essential exercise is to encourage teachers, school counselors, administrators, and other school personnel to imagine what the ideal school should or can be (Davis & Osborn, 1999). This exercise is similar to the Miracle Question, and is one example of other future-oriented exception questions discussed in chapter 4. Although such a strategy was discussed in relation to school counselors' work with students, it is vitally important that all solution-focused exercises not be confined or thought of exclusively in regard to their use with students. Doing so limits the benefit of solution-focused school counseling and precludes the creation of a solution-focused school.

So . . . imagine what your school would be like if its present concerns and troubling issues no longer existed. If these current complaints magically or miraculously disappeared, what would be left? What would you see enduring in their place?

In order to appreciate the full extent of this exercise, first identify what you would consider to be the most nerve-wracking, stress-inducing, energy-sapping, or debilitating aspect of your current position or school. What is in your estimation, not as it *should* be, at your school? As much as you would prefer to do otherwise, hold that (unpleasant and discomforting!) thought for a brief moment. Do you have it identified? Once you do, and just as quickly as it came to your mind, envision the immediate, decisive, and swift disappearance of that negative aspect. Poof!

What would your school be like in the wake of its disappearance? What would be the first thing for you to notice about what you identified as debilitating and negative no longer being there? What would the teachers notice? What would the students notice as being different? What would the parents notice first? What would the principal and other school administrators detect as being different? What would be some of the small signs suggesting progress was being made toward the realization of the desired school?

These presuppositional questions, by definition, have imbedded within them the assumption that change will occur and is, in fact, already happening. These types of questions help school personnel reframe their thinking towards what works. More often than not, the school envisioned in the preceding exercise already exists. Yes, this is true! Granted, it does not exist all the time or in the full measure you imagined, but it does currently exist. This is to say that the ingredients for the ideal or "miracle" school you pictured do *already* exist—they may just need to be recognized and cultivated.

From a solution-focused perspective, carefully identifying and cultivating such solution or "miracle" ingredients is the key to creating a solution-focused school. The benefits of the future-oriented exercise are realized when school staff are encouraged to amplify the exceptions to the problem or debilitating school. "Doing more of what is already working" is an important step toward realizing the solution-focused school.

☐ Teaching the Teachers

Teaching the Teachers "Solution Talk"

Imagining the ideal school not only implies a shift in thinking; it carries with it the need for new language. To a great extent, the words we choose to envision and describe the ideal school represent our commitment to making such a working environment a reality. "It'll never happen," "Dream on," and "But we've always done it this way" signify a lack of investment in the process of positive change. Words carry meaning and serve to convey the speaker's intentions. Speaking a new, non-problem focused language is key in the construction of a solution-focused school.

Specific words, such as "instead" and "different" can be inserted in conversations with teachers about their students on a regular basis.

- "What *differences* have you noticed in Anne since she came down and talked with me last week?"
- "What needs to happen *instead* of conflicting with class time for this support group to form and get off the ground?"
- "Tell me how you *managed* to keep things from getting out of hand."
- "What things do you see him doing *differently* that tell you he's really trying this week?"

A similar language can be adopted with parents and school administrators. Imagine a staff meeting with other school personnel wherein the following observations and questions are expressed:

- "*When* our proficiency test scores reach the acceptable level next year, what do you think we could say was the number one thing we did to account for the climb?"

- "What will need to happen to *convince* school board members that the sex education seminar we ran last year was effective and is worth doing again?"
- "I believe Dominic has demonstrated an outstanding effort during his probationary period to warrant his reinstatement on student council. I suggest we recognize him in some way for getting *back on track.*"
- "Okay, so we didn't hit the bull's eye with our 'Parents as Partners' campaign. Let's talk for a moment, though, about what we did and what happened that came *in the vicinity of* our targeted goal."

Words that convey positive presuppositions, such as *"When* our proficiency scores begin to rise," are highlighted in solution-focused talk. In addition, words that represent efforts to manage difficulties, get back on track, or come close to reaching a monumental goal are emphasized. Such language draws attention to success stories that are in the making, solutions that are percolating, and it validates efforts currently being made, rather than commiserating over failure or obsessing about perfection. The intention is *not* to hit the bull's eye, rather, it's to be in the vicinity.

Solution talk, therefore, often captures effort or movement, not necessarily the "perfect" outcome or final product. Walter and Peller (1994) illustrated this in their discussion of the "on track" metaphor in solution-focused counseling: "Our belief is that therapy is about getting *on track* with living normal processes—not about solving, changing, or completing the process" (p. 114).

Solution-focused words are intentionally used, therefore, to capture what lies in between extreme polarities, not just either–or ways of thinking. Events that could be considered in between a worst case scenario and an instantaneous cure are given attention; efforts undertaken that represent neither a total disaster nor a miraculous occurrence are highlighted and verbalized. "What will Alisha be doing when you sense that she is *beginning* to make *some progress*?" is an example of a solution-focused perspective, in contrast to the problem-focused observation, "Alisha is *never* going to graduate!"

Solution talk captures and conveys possibility and progress. The words describe something other than catastrophe or helplessness. If change is always happening, as one of the solution-focused principles makes clear, then our language must illustrate such change. And once select words such as "instead" and "notice the difference" are used around the school with students and with staff, a funny thing happens: ears perk up and thinking begins to shift from problem to possibility. Just like the domino or ripple effect—one carefully selected solution-focused word can make the difference in a school atmosphere.

The school counselor can be the primary facilitator for teachers who are wishing to become solution-focused in their work. Given the fact that counselors are often short on time and long on tasks, it is wise to enlist teachers as front line interventionists. Ajmal and Rhodes (1995) described their consultative work with teachers as conversations consisting primarily of questions, which they say makes use of the limited time they have to converse during the course of a hectic school day. They state that

> by using questions which encourage a focus on next steps, first signs of progress, what would people like to happen differently, even a 10 minute talk can be used to good effect, so that the teacher has something to take away and try. (p. 20)

Teaching teachers the basic concepts of solution-focused interventions aids the teacher by offering a practical system of addressing student concerns. Teachers with classroom management problems, for example, are ones who can benefit from a solution-focused philosophy of working with students (Osenton & Chang, 1999). In this regard, it is often the teacher who is the "client" for the intervention (Durrant, 1995). As teachers learn how to work with students with their own challenges and problems, they are also learning methods and techniques that they can employ as they struggle with addressing classroom challenges. Table 6.1 offers a basic outline for school counselors to use who are interested in offering an in-service to teachers on becoming solution-focused. Although not intended to be comprehensive, following a program such as this will offer teachers the basic tools to employ these principles in their classrooms.

Think Exceptions

Discovering how solutions are already occurring is the key to "thinking exceptions." Encouraging school staff to look for those moments when things are going well will move the school toward being solution-focused. Finding such exceptions can be challenging—we have a tendency to get stuck in a problem focus. When past, present, or future (i.e., imagined) exceptions to current problems are identified, however, we instill hope and encouragement in those seeking our assistance.

Optimum System Products, Inc., a private business that services banks nationwide and has its headquarters in Columbus, Ohio, has established its own procedure for encouraging the detection of exceptional behavior among its employees. "**C**atching **O**thers **P**erforming **S**uccess-

Table 6.1. Teacher in-service solution-focused strategies for teachers

The purpose of this workshop is to familiarize classroom teachers with solution-focused strategies that a teacher might use in the classroom, or working individually with students, parents, or other school personnel. Reference has been made to specific chapters within this book to assist the school counselor in organizing information for their in-service.

A. An introduction to being solution-focused in the classroom.

* Offer examples of how we can be overwhelmed by "problems", and how they can begin searching for what is working in those situations (see chapter 1).

B. Moving from problems to solutions, what's the difference?

* Explain and offer examples of how the classroom teacher can shift their mind set from one of problem focus to solution-focus (see chapter 3).

C. Adopting a presuppositional point of view.

* Change is always happening. Address how the students will benefit when the teacher reflect and highlights exceptions to the students problems (see chapter 4).

D. Helping students to think "what if" in the classroom. How the teacher can use the Miracle Question.

* Offer teachers examples of how they can assist students by identifying what it would be like if "the problem was not there" (see chapter 4).

E. Self-help for the teacher. Adopting the "Great Instead" philosophy.

* Address how the teacher can apply these concepts to themselves by thinking about what they would like to happen instead of the current problem issue in the classroom (see chapter 4).

F. Employing Solution-Focused strategies in Parent-Teacher conferences.

* Focus on how the teacher can enlist the parent as a partner in working with their children (see chapter 5).

fully," or COPS for short, is a program in which personnel accrue "points" each time a peer "catches" them doing something note-worthy, such as following up with a customer to verify product and delivery satisfaction or launching the new web page ahead of schedule. The employee with the most number of COPS points reported by peers at the end of the year is entitled to a unique bonus, such as an all-expense-paid trip for their family to the Rockies or Ireland. Imagine working in such an environment wherein colleagues pay attention and report what's going well, rather than on problems! Imagine the school wherein counselors, teachers, administrators, and other staff were to invest in such a COPS program!

Bear in mind that exceptions are naturally occurring examples of things going well. Solutions are always taking place. It may be easier, therefore, to build on existing positive behaviors than to attempt to build new ones. One doesn't have to teach an old dog new tricks if the old tricks can be modified and built upon to work (Kral, 1995).

A Vision of the Possible

The "exceptional" solution-focused school is a collaborative effort and an integrated phenomenon. This means that all personnel, not just the counseling staff, share a similar vision of what the solution-focused school will be. They also work together to usher in the realization of such a competency-based environment—a learning environment that, furthermore, does not segregate the academic from the emotional demands of its students. As Ames and Miller (1994) have observed, "You cannot separate social and emotional development from intellectual development or affective education from academic achievement; they are inextricably intertwined" (p. 100).

Ames and Miller (1994) recommended "personalizing the middle school experience" (p. 2), wherein, among other characteristics, a range of support services are available that address students' needs. In addition, strong links among family, school, and community are established "so that all work in harmony to support children's development" (p. 3). This vision is similar to the one proposed by Dryfoos (1994) in her description of full-service schools wherein "a new kind of 'seamless' institution, a community-oriented school with a joint governance structure that allows maximum responsiveness to the community" (p. 12) is established.

The exceptional solution-focused school represents a collaborative effort and an integration of services, both within the school and in the community. The cooperation of all school personnel is essential. Mostert et al. (1997) proposed that "training other school professionals in the [solution-focused] model could significantly reduce the amount of time devoted to interprofessional conflict and the common consequent delay in problem solving for the good of the client" (p. 24).

The exceptional solution-focused school, however, begins with the vision of the school counselor—a vision of what is possible. Anderson and Reiter (1995) alluded to this in their description of the counselor as futurist, one of seven characteristics of the "indispensable counselor." They stated that

> indispensable, futuristic counselors change to meet changing client demands; depend on research, but are alert to trends before the research findings reach the schools; and have a clear vision of what the counseling program can be to prepare students for their world. (p. 275)

The rudimentary efforts of establishing an exceptional solution-focused school, therefore, rest with the school counselor. Recognizing and itemizing the strengths of your current school is a first step. Communicating these positive attributes with students and staff is a second step. Also, an open dialogue with students, teachers, parents, principals and other school personnel, and school board members about what the school *can be,* is an additional step.

Your vision of your current school as an exceptional solution-focused one matters. Envisioning such a school implies hope, and hope breeds enthusiasm, which leads to energy invested in action. Envision for your school what you wish and dream for your students:

- strength in the midst of turmoil
- clear thinking and careful decision-making
- discarding stagnant and ineffective ways of doing things
- adopting more healthy, balanced, and productive behaviors
- a desire and an ability to work as a team player
- investment in the well-being of others and one's community
- genuine pride and confidence in one's strengths and abilities

Such a vision may very well determine the life and health of your school. To paraphrase an Old Testament proverb, "where there is no vision, the school will perish" (Proverbs 29:18). A vision of the possible, therefore, is the guiding force and anchor for the exceptional solution-focused school.

☐ Summary

Solution-focused counseling is a method of intervention being successfully employed in school and in other public and private settings. A foundation of this approach is the assumption that counseling and other professional interactions are often brief in nature and, therefore, need a clear focus. In addition, the approach assumes that change is inevitable and constant, and that there are always exceptions to problems.

These assumptions provide a useful framework for the school counselor and represent a positive, hopeful, and beneficial paradigm for other personnel within the school system. A solution-focused school, guided by exception-finding and exception-enhancing counselors and other school staff, is an exceptional model.

REFERENCES

Ajmal, Y., & Rhodea, J. (1995). Solution-focused brief therapy, EPs and schools. *Educational and Child Psychology, 12*(4), 16–21.

Amatea, E. S. (1988). Engaging the reluctant client: Some new strategies for the school counselor. *The School Counselor, 36*, 34–40.

Amatea, E. S. (1989). *Brief strategic intervention for school behavior problems.* San Francisco: Jossey-Bass.

Amatea, E. S., & Sherrard, P. A. D. (1991). When students cannot or will not change their behavior: Using brief strategic intervention in the school. *Journal of Counseling and Development, 69*, 341–344.

Ames, N. L., & Miller, E. (1994). *Changing middle schools: How to make schools work for young adolescents.* San Francisco: Jossey-Bass.

Anderson, H., & Goolishian, H. (1991). Thinking about multi-agency work with substance abusers and their families: A language systems approach. *Journal of Strategic and Systemic Therapies, 10*, 20–35.

Anderson, R. S., & Reiter, D. (1995). The indispensable counselor. *The School Counselor, 42*, 268–276.

Baker, S. (1996). *School counseling for the 21st century* (2nd ed.). Englewood Cliffs, NJ: Prentice Hall.

Barletta, J. (1998). A solution-focused approach to time limited counselling. *Australian Journal of Guidance and Counselling, 8*, 105–110

Beale, A. V. (1995). Selecting school counselors: The principal's perspective. *The School Counselor, 42*, 211–217.

Berg, I. K. (1994). *Family-based services: A solution-focused approach.* New York: Norton.

Berg, I. K. (1995). Solution-focused brief counseling with substance abusers. In A. M. Washton (Ed.), *Psychotherapy and substance abuse: A practitioner's handbook* (pp. 223–242). New York: Guilford.

Berg, I. K., & de Shazer, S. (1993). Making numbers talk: Language in counseling. In S. Friedman (Ed.), *The new language of change: Constructive collaboration in psychotherapy* (pp. 5–24). New York: Guilford.

Berg, I. K., & Miller, S. D. (1992a). *Working with the problem drinker: A solution-focused approach.* New York: Norton.

Berg, I. K., & Miller, S. D. (1992b). Working with Asian American clients: One person at a time. *Families in Society: The Journal of Contemporary Human Services, 73*, 356–363.

Biever, J. L., McKenzie, K., Wales-North, M., & Gonzalez, R. C. (1995). Stories and solutions in psychotherapy with adolescents. *Adolescence, 30*(118), 491–499.

Bloom, B. L. (1992). Planned short-term psychotherapy: Current status and future challenges. *Applied and Preventive Psychology, 1*, 157–164.

Bloom, B. L. (1997). *Planned short-term psychotherapy: A clinical handbook* (2nd ed.). Boston: Allyn and Bacon.

Bohart, A. C., & Tallman, K. (1999). *How clients make therapy work: The process of active self-healing.* Washington, DC: American Psychological Association.

Brasher, B., Campbell, T. C., & Moen, D. (1993). Solution oriented recovery. *Journal of Systemic Therapies, 12*(3), 1–14.

Bray, M. A., & Kehle, T. J. (1996). Self-modeling as an intervention for stuttering. *School Psychology Review, 25,* 358–369.

Bruce, M. A., & Hopper, G. C. (1997). Brief counseling versus traditional counseling: A comparison of effectiveness. *The School Counselor, 44,* 171–184.

Bruce, M.A. (1995). Brief counseling: An effective model for change. *The School Counselor, 42,* 353–363.

Budman, S. H., & Gurman, A. S. (1988). *Theory and practice of brief counseling.* New York: Guilford.

Cade, B., & O'Hanlon, W. H. (1993). *A brief guide to brief counseling.* New York: Norton.

Campbell, J., Elder, J., Gallagher, D., Simon, J., & Taylor, A. (1999). Crafting the "tap on the shoulder:" A compliment template for solution-focused therapy. *American Journal of Family Therapy, 27,* 35–47.

Chang, J. (1998). Children's stories, children's solutions: Social constructionist therapy for children and their families. In M. F. Hoyt (Ed.), *The handbook of constructive therapies: Innovative approaches from leading practitioners* (pp. 251–275). San Francisco: Jossey-Bass.

Cooper, J. F. (1995). *A primer of brief psychotherapy.* New York: Norton.

Corcoran, J. (1997). A solution-oriented approach to working with juvenile offenders. *Child and Adolescent Social Work Journal, 14,* 277–288.

Corey, G. (1996). *Theory and practice of counseling and psychotherapy* (5th ed.). Pacific Grove, CA: Brooks/Cole.

Coy, D. R. (1999). The role and training of the school counselor: Background and purpose. *National Association of Secondary School Principals Bulletin, 83*(603), 2–8.

Cross, C. D. (1995). Organizing group psychotherapy programming in managed care settings. In K. R. MacKenzie (Ed.), *Effective use of group counseling in managed care* (pp. 27–41). Washington, DC: American Psychiatric Press.

Cummings, N. A. (1995). Impact of managed care on employment and training: A primer for survival. *Professional Psychology: Research and Practice, 26,* 10–15.

Davis, T. E., & Osborn, C. J. (1999). The solution-focused school: An exceptional model. *National Association of Secondary School Principals Bulletin, 83,* 40–46.

De Jong, P., & Berg, I. K. (1998). *Interviewing for solutions.* Pacific Grove, CA: Brooks/Cole.

De Jong, P., & Hopwood, L. E. (1996). Outcome research on treatment conducted at the Brief Family Therapy Center, 1992–1993. In S. D. Miller, M. A. Hubble, & B. L. Duncan (Eds.), *Handbook of solution-focused brief therapy* (pp. 272–298). San Francisco: Jossey-Bass.

de Shazer, S. (1985). *Key to solutions in brief therapy.* New York: Norton.

de Shazer, S. (1988). *Clues: Investigating solutions in brief therapy.* New York: Norton.

de Shazer, S. (1990). Brief therapy. In J. K. Zeig & W. M. Munion (Eds.), *What is psychotherapy? Contemporary perspectives* (pp. 278–282). San Francisco: Jossey-Bass.

de Shazer, S. (1991). *Putting difference to work.* New York: Norton.

de Shazer, S. (1994). *Words were originally magic.* New York: Norton.

de Shazer, S., & Berg, I. K. (1992). Doing counseling: A post-structural re-vision. *Journal of Marital and Family Counseling, 18,* 71–81.

de Shazer, S., Berg, I. K., Lipchik, E., Nunnally, E., Molnar, A., Gingerich, W., & Weiner Davis, M. (1986). Brief counseling: Focused solution development. *Family Process, 25,* 207–221.

Donovan, J. M. (1987). Brief dynamic psychotherapy: Toward a more comprehensive model. *Psychiatry, 50,* 167–183.

Downing, J., & Harrison, T. (1992). Solutions and school counseling. *The School Counselor, 39,* 327–332.

Dreikeurs, R. (1964). *Children: The challenge.* New York: Hawthorn.

Dryfoos, J. G. (1994). *Full-service schools: A revolution in health and social services for children, youth, and families.* San Francisco: Jossey-Bass.

Duncan, B. L., & Moynihan, D. W. (1994). Applying outcome research: Intentional utilization of the client's frame of reference. *Psychotherapy, 31,* 294–301.

Durrant, M. (1995). *Creative strategies for school problems: Solutions for psychologists and teachers.* New York: Norton.

Eckert, P. A. (1993). Acceleration of change: Catalysts in brief counseling. *Clinical Psychology Review, 13,* 241–253.

Edelstien, M. G. (1990). *Symptom analysis: A method of brief counseling.* New York: Norton.

Erickson, M. H. (1954). Special techniques of brief hypnotherapy. *Journal of Clinical and Experimental Hypnosis, 2,* 109–129.

Fish, J. M. (1997). Paradox for complainants? Strategic thoughts about solution-focused therapy. *Journal of Systemic Therapies, 16,* 266–273.

Franklin, C., Corcoran, J., Nowicki, J., & Streeter, C. (1997). Using client self-anchored scales to measure outcomes in solution-focused therapy. *Journal of Systemic Therapies, 16,* 246–265.

Furman, B., & Ahola, T. (1995). Solution talk: The solution-oriented way of talking about problems. In M. F. Hoyt (Ed.), *Constructive therapies* (pp. 41–66). New York: Guilford.

Garfield, S. L. (1994). Research on client variables in psychotherapy. In A. E. Bergin & S. L. Garfield (Eds.), *Handbook of psychotherapy and behavior change* (4th ed., pp. 190–228). New York: Wiley.

Gingerich, W. J., de Shazer, S., & Weiner-Davis, M. (1988). Constructing change: A research view of interviewing. In E. Lipchik (Ed.), *Interviewing* (pp. 21–32). Rockville, MD: Aspen.

Greene, G. J., Lee, M. Y., Mentzer, R. A., Pinnel, S. R., & Niles, D. (1998). Miracles, dreams, and empowerment: A brief therapy practice of note. *Families in Society, 79,* 395–399.

Gysbers, N. C., & Henderson, P. (1994). *Developing and managing your school guidance program* (2nd ed.). Alexandria, VA: American Counseling Association.

Haley, J. (1990). Why not long-term counseling? In J. K. Zeig & S. G. Gilligan (Eds.), *Brief counseling: Myths, methods, and metaphors* (pp. 3–17). New York: Brunner/Mazel.

Hopwood, L., & Taylor, M. (1993). Solution-focused brief therapy for chronic problems. In I. VanderCreek, S. Knapp, & T. L. Jackson (Eds.), *Innovations in clinical practice: A sourcebook, Vol. 12* (pp. 85–97). Sarasota, FL: Professional Resource Press/Professional Resource Exchange.

Howard, K. I., Kopta, S. M., Krause, M. S., & Orlinsky, D. E. (1986). The dose-effect relationship in psychotherapy. *American Psychologist, 41,* 159–164.

Howard, K. I., Lueger, R. J., Maling, M. S., & Martinovich, Z. (1993). A phase model of psychotherapy outcome: Causal mediation of change. *Journal of Consulting and Clinical Psychology, 61,* 678–685.

Hoyt, M. F. (1991). Teaching and learning short-term psychotherapy. In C. S. Austad & W. H. Berman (Eds.), *Psychotherapy in managed health care: The optimal use of time and resources* (pp. 98–107). Washington, DC: American Psychological Association.

Hoyt, M. F. (1994). Characteristics of psychotherapy under managed behavioral healthcare. *Behavioral Healthcare Tomorrow,* September/October, 59–62.

Hoyt, M. F. (1995). Brief psychotherapies. In A. S. Gurman & S. B. Messer (Eds.), *Essential psychotherapies: Theories and practice* (pp. 441–487). New York: Guilford.

Kaplan, L. S. (1995). Principals versus counselors: Resolving tensions from different practice models. *The School Counselor, 42*, 261–267.

Keys, S. G., Bemak, F., & Lockhart, E. J. (1998). Transforming school counseling to serve the mental health needs of at-risk youth. *Journal of Counseling and Development, 76*, 381–388.

Kiser, D. J., & Nunnally, E. (1990). The relationship between treatment length and goal achievement in solution-focused brief therapy. Unpublished manuscript.

Kopta, S. M., Howard, K. I., Lowry, J. L., & Beutler, L. E. (1994). Patterns of symptomatic recovery in psychotherapy. *Journal of Consulting and Clinical Psychology, 62*, 1009–1016.

Koss, M. P., & Butcher, J. N. (1986). Research on brief psychotherapy. In S. L. Garfield & A. E. Bergin (Eds.), *Handbook of psychotherapy and behavior change* (3rd ed., pp. 627–670). New York: Wiley.

Koss, M. P., & Shiang, J. (1994). Research on brief psychotherapy. In A. E. Bergin & S. L. Garfield (Eds.), *Handbook of psychotherapy and behavior change* (4th ed., pp. 664–700). New York: Wiley.

Kottler, J. A. (1997). *Succeeding with difficult students.* Thousand Oaks, CA: Corwin Press.

Kovacs, A. L. (1982). Survival in the 1980s: On the theory and practice of brief psychotherapy. *Psychotherapy: Theory, Research and Practice, 19*, 142–159.

Kral, R. (1987). Getting ahead by turning 180 degrees: Brief counseling in the public schools. Paper presented at the National Association for School Psychologists' Convention, March, 1987.

Kral, R. (1995). *Strategies that work: Techniques for solutions in schools.* Milwaukee, WI: Brief Family Therapy Center Press.

Kral, R., & Kowalski, K. (1989). After the miracle: The second stage in solution focused brief therapy. *Journal of Strategic and Systemic Therapies, 8*, 73–76.

LaFountain, R. M., Garner, N. E., & Eliason, G. T. (1996). Solution-focused counseling groups: A key for school counselors. *The School Counselor, 43*, 256–267.

Lambert, M. J. (1992). Implications of outcome research for psychotherapy integration. In J. C. Norcross & M. R. Goldfried (Eds.), *Handbook of psychotherapy integration* (pp. 94–129). New York: BasicBooks.

Lambert, M. J., & Bergin, A. E. (1994). The effectiveness of psychotherapy. In A. E. Bergin & S. L. Garfield (Eds.), *Handbook of psychotherapy and behavior change* (4th ed., pp. 143–190). New York: Wiley.

Lambert, M. J., Okiishi, J. C., Finch, A. E., & Johnson, L. D. (1998). Outcome assessment: From conceptualization to implementation. *Professional Psychology: Research and Practice, 29*, 63–70.

Lavoritano, J. E., & Segal, P. B. (1992). Evaluating the efficacy of short-term counseling on adolescents in a school setting. *Adolescence, 27*, 555–543.

Lawson, D. (1994). Identifying pretreatment change. *Journal of Counseling and Development, 72*, 244–248.

Lazarus, A. A., & Fay. A. (1990). Brief psychotherapy: Tautology or oxymoron? In J. K. Zeig & S. G. Gilligan (Eds.), *Brief counseling: Myths, methods, and metaphors* (pp. 36–51). New York: Brunner/Mazel.

Lee, C.C. (1995) *Counseling for diversity.* Needham Heights: Allyn and Bacon.

Lee, M. Y. (1998). A study of solution-focused brief family therapy: Outcomes and issues. *The American Journal of Family Therapy, 25*, 3–17.

Levenson, H., Speed, J., & Budman, S. H. (1995). Therapist's experience, training, and skill in brief counseling: A bicoastal survey. *American Journal of Psychotherapy, 49*, 95–117.

Lipchik, E. (1994). The rush to be brief. *Networker*, March/April, 35–39.

Littrell, J. M. (1998). *Brief counseling in action*. New York: Norton.

Littrell, J. M., Malia, J. A., Nichols, R., Olson, J., Nesselhuf, D., & Crandell, P. (1992). Brief counseling: Helping counselors adopt an innovative counseling approach. *The School Counselor, 39,* 171–175.

Littrell, J. M., Malia, J. A., & Vanderwood, M. (1995). Single-session brief counseling in a high school. *Journal of Counseling and Development, 73,* 451–457.

McFarland, B. (1995). *Brief counseling and eating disorders: A practical guide to solution-focused work with clients.* San Francisco: Jossey-Bass.

McGarty, R. (1985). Relevance of Ericksonian psychotherapy to the treatment of chemical dependency. *Journal of Substance Abuse Treatment, 2,* 147–151.

McKeel, A. J. (1996). A clinician's guide to research on solution-focused brief therapy. In S. D. Miller, M. A. Hubble, & B. L. Duncan (Eds.), *Handbook of solution-focused brief therapy* (pp. 251–271). New York: Wiley.

Metcalf, L. (1995). *Counseling towards solutions: A practical solution-focused program for working with students, teachers, and parents.* West Nyack, NY: The Center for Applied Research in Education.

Metcalf, L. (1998). *Solution focused group therapy: Ideas for groups in private practice, schools, agencies, and treatment programs.* New York: The Free Press.

Miller, G. (1997). Systems and solutions: The discourses of brief therapy. *Contemporary Family Therapy, 19,* 5–22.

Miller, S. D. (1992). The symptoms of solution. *Journal of Strategic and Systemic Therapies, 11,* 1–11.

Miller, S. D. (1994). The solution conspiracy: A mystery in three installments. *Journal of Systemic Therapies, 13,* 18–37.

Miller, W. R., Benefield, R. G., & Tonigan, J. S. (1993). Enhancing motivation for change in problem drinking: A controlled comparison of two therapist styles. *Journal of Consulting and Clinical Psychology, 61,* 455–461.

Miller, W. R., & Rollnick, S. (1991). *Motivational interviewing: Preparing people to change addictive behavior.* New York: Guilford.

Miller, W. R., & Sovereign, R. G. (1989). The check-up: A model for early intervention in addictive behaviors. In T. Loberg, W. R. Miller, P. E. Nathan, & G. A. Marlatt (Eds.), *Addictive behaviors: Prevention and early intervention* (pp. 219–231). Amsterdam: Swef & Zeitlinger.

Miller, W. R., Zweben, A., DiClemente, C. C., & Rychtarik, R. G. (1992). *Motivational enhancement therapy manual: A clinical research guide for therapists treating individuals with alcohol abuse and dependence.* Rockville, MD: National Institute on Alcohol and Alcoholism.

Molnar, A., & de Shazer, S. (1987). Solution-focused therapy: Toward the identification of therapeutic tasks. *Journal of Marital and Family Therapy, 13,* 349–358.

Mostert, D. L., Johnson, E., & Mostert, M. P. (1997). The utility of solution-focused, brief counseling in schools: Potential from an initial study. *Professional School Counseling, 1,* 21–24.

Murphy, J. J. (1997). *Solution-focused counseling in middle and high schools.* Alexandria, VA: American Counseling Association.

Murstein, B. I. (1963). *Theory and research in projective techniques, emphasizing the TAT.* New York: Wiley.

Nelson, V. (1998). Notice the difference. *Journal of Family Psychotherapy, 9,* 81–84.

Nunnally, E. (1993). Solution focused therapy. In R. A. Wells and V. J. Giannetti (Eds.), *Casebook of the brief psychotherapies* (pp. 271–286). New York: Plenum.

Nylund, D., & Corsiglia, V. (1994). Becoming solution-forced in brief therapy: Remembering something important we already knew. *Journal of Systemic Therapies, 13,* 5–12.

O'Hanlon, W., & Weiner-Davis, M. (1989). *In search of solutions: A new direction in psychotherapy.* New York: Norton.

Orlinsky, D. E., Grawe, K., & Parks, B. K. (1994). Process and outcome in psychotherapy C Noch einmal. In A. E. Bergin & S. L. Garfield (Eds.), *Handbook of psychotherapy and behavior change* (4th ed., pp. 270–376). New York: Wiley.

Osborn, C. J. (1996). Solution-focused brief counseling in alcoholism treatment: The impact of clinicians' views of alcoholism (Doctoral dissertation, Ohio University, 1996). *Dissertation Abstracts International, 57-04*, 1503.

Osborn, C. J. (1999). Solution-focused strategies with 'involuntary' clients: Practical applications for the school and clinical settings. *Journal of Humanistic Education and Development, 37*, 169–181.

Osenton, T., & Chang, J. (1999). Solution-oriented classroom management: A proactive application with young children. *Journal of Systemic Therapies, 18*, 65–76.

Patterson, G. R., & Forgatch, M. S. (1985). Therapist behavior as a determinant for client noncompliance: A paradox for the behavior modifier. *Journal of Consulting and Clinical Psychology, 53*, 846–851.

Prochaska, J. O., DiClemente, C. C., & Norcross, J. C. (1992). In search of how people change: Applications to addictive behaviors. *American Psychologist, 47*, 1102–1114.

Quick, E. K. (1996). *Doing what works in brief therapy: A strategic solution focused approach.* San Diego, CA: Academic Press.

Ritchie, M. H. (1994). Counselling difficult children. *Canadian Journal of Counselling, 28*, 58–68.

Santa Rita, E., Jr. (1998). What do you do after asking the miracle question in solution-focused therapy? *Family Therapy, 25*, 189–195.

Sears, S. J. (1993). The changing scope of practice of the secondary school counselor. *The School Counselor, 40*, 384–388.

Selekman, M. (1991). The solution-oriented parenting group: A treatment alternative that works. *Journal of Strategic and Systemic Therapies, 10*, 36–49.

Selekman, M. D. (1993). *Pathways to change: Brief therapy solutions with difficult adolescents.* New York: Guilford.

Seligman, M. E. P. (1991). *Learned optimism.* New York: Knopf.

Sergiovanni, T. J. (1994). *Building community in schools.* San Francisco: Jossey-Bass.

Sexton, T. L., & Whiston, S. C. (1994). The status of the counseling relationship: An empirical review, theoretical implications, and research directions. *The Counseling Psychologist, 22*, 6–78.

Sexton, T. L., Whiston, S. C., Bleuer, J. C., & Walz, G. R. (1997). *Integrating outcome research into counseling practice and training.* Alexandria, VA: American Counseling Association.

Shoham, V., Rohrbaugh, M., & Patterson, J. (1995). Problem- and solution-focused couple therapies: The MRI and Milwaukee models. In N. S. Jacobson & A. E. Gurman (Eds.), *Clinical handbook of couple therapy* (pp. 142–163). New York: Guilford.

Short, P. M., & Greer, J. T. (1997). *Leadership in empowered schools: Themes from innovative efforts.* Columbus, OH: Prentice Hall.

Sklare, G. B. (1997). *Brief counseling that works: A solution-focused approach for school counselors.* Thousand Oaks, CA: Corwin.

Smith, M. L., Glass, G. V., & Miller, T. I. (1980). *The benefits of psychotherapy.* Baltimore: Johns Hopkins University Press.

Steenbarger, B. N. (1992). Toward science-practice integration in brief counseling and counseling. *The Counseling Psychologist, 20*, 403–450.

Steenbarger, B. N. (1994). Duration and outcome in psychotherapy: An integrative review. *Professional Psychology: Research and Practice, 25*, 111–119.

Stein, D. M., & lambert, M. J. (1995). Graduate training in psychotherapy: Are therapy outcomes enhanced? *Journal of Consulting and Clinical Psychology, 63*, 182–196.

Stern, S. (1993). Managed care, brief counseling, and therapeutic integrity. *Psychotherapy, 30*, 162–175.

Strupp, H. H. (1995). Foreword. In H. L. Levenson, *Time-limited dynamic psychotherapy: A guide to clinical practice* (pp. ix–xi). New York: BasicBooks/Harper Collins.

Sullivan, H. S. (1954). *The psychiatric review*. New York: Norton.

Tallman, K., & Bohart, A. C. (1999). The client as a common factor: Clients as self-healers. In M. A. Hubble, B. L. Duncan, & S. D. Miller (Eds.), *The heart and soul of change: What works in therapy* (pp. 91–131). Washington, DC: American Psychological Association.

Talmon, M. (1990). *Single-session therapy: Maximizing the effect of the first (and often only) therapeutic encounter*. San Francisco: Jossey-Bass.

Walter, J. L., & Peller, J. E. (1992). *Becoming solution-focused in brief counseling*. New York: Brunner/Mazel.

Walter, J. L., & Peller, J. E. (1994). 'On track' in solution-focused brief therapy. In M. F. Hoyt (Ed.), *Constructive therapies* (pp. 111–125). New York: Guilford.

Weiner-Davis, M., de Shazer, S., & Gingerich, W. J. (1987). Using pretreatment change to construct a therapeutic solution: An exploratory study. *Journal of Marital and Family Therapy, 13*, 359–363.

Wells, R. A. (1993). Clinical strategies in brief psychotherapy. In R. A. Wells & V. J. Gianetti (Eds.), *Casebook of the brief psychotherapies* (pp. 3–17). New York: Plenum.

Wells, R. A., & Phelps, P. A. (1990). The brief psychotherapies: A selective overview. In R. Wells & V. Gianetti (Eds.), *Handbook of brief psychotherapies* (pp. 3–26). New York: Plenum.

INDEX